JEFFREY H. HACKER

CARL SANDBURG

FRANKLIN WATTS
NEW YORK I LONDON I TORONTO I SYDNEY I 1984
AN IMPACT BIOGRAPHY

A GROLIER COMPANY

Cover photograph courtesy of Culver Pictures.

Photographs courtesy of: "Leviton-Atlanta" from Black Star: p. 7; Carl Sandburg Collection, University of Illinois Library, Urbana-Champaign: pp. 25, 40, 43; The Bettmann Archive: pp. 60, 70; Wide World: pp. 88, 106; UPI: p. 99; Dan J. McCoy from Black Star: p. 114.

ACKNOWLEDGMENTS

For permission to reprint copyrighted material, grateful acknowledgment is made to Harcourt Brace Jovanovich, Inc. for the following poems: "Fog," "The Harbor," "Style," "Boes," "Chicago," "Masses," and "Fish Crier" from *Chicago Poems* by Carl Sandburg, copyright © 1916 by Holt, Rinehart and Winston, Inc., copyright © 1944 by Carl Sandburg. Reprinted by permission of Harcourt Brace Jovanovich, Inc.: "Wanderin' " from *The American Songbag* by Carl Sandburg, copyright © 1927 by Harcourt Brace Jovanovich, Inc., copyright © 1955 by Carl Sandburg. Reprinted by permission of the publisher: "Prairie," "Autumn Movement," and "Grass" from *Cornhuskers* by Carl Sandburg, copyright © 1918 by Holt, Rinehart and Winston, Inc., copyright © 1946 by Carl Sandburg. Reprinted by permission of Harcourt Brace Jovanovich, Inc.: "Smoke and Steel," and "Purple Martins" from *Smoke and Steel* by Carl Sandburg, copyright © 1920 by Harcourt Brace Jovanovich, Inc., copyright © 1948 by Carl Sandburg. Reprinted by permission of the publisher: "Good Morning, America" from *Good Morning, America,* copyright © 1956 by Carl Sandburg. Reprinted by permission of Harcourt Brace Jovanovich, Inc.: "The People, Yes" from *The People, Yes* by Carl Sandburg, copyright © 1936 by Harcourt Brace Jovanovich, Inc., copyright © 1964 by Carl Sandburg. Reprinted by permission of the publisher: "Timesweep" copyright © 1953, copyright © 1963 by Carl Sandburg. Reprinted from *The Complete Poems of Carl Sandburg* by permission of Harcourt Brace Jovanovich, Inc.

Library of Congress Cataloging in Publication Data

Hacker, Jeffrey H.
Carl Sandburg.

(An impact biography)
Bibliography: p.
Includes index.
Summary: The life of the American poet, biographer, and collector of folk songs whose biography of Lincoln took twenty years of research and writing.
1. Sandburg, Carl, 1878-1967—Juvenile literature.
2. Poets, American—20th century—Biography—Juvenile literature.
1. Sandburg, Carl, 1878-1967. 2. Poets, American] I. title.
PS3537.A618Z594 1984   811'.52 [B] [92]   83-23328
ISBN 0-531-04762-8

CONTENTS

To Mark
and Rick:
"young strangers,
coming"

"Here or there you may witness a startling harmony
where you say, 'This will be haunting me a long time
with a loveliness I hope to understand better.' "

CARL SANDBURG,
Prologue to *The Family of Man*

ECHO OF THE PEOPLE

1

A broad-shouldered Chicago newspaperman sat in the ante-room of a courthouse, waiting to interview the judge. For the energetic, hard-hitting columnist of *The Day Book*, a small leftist tabloid, it was a rare moment of quiet. When he wasn't writing articles on the ills of society, he was giving speeches on the plight of the working class, helping organize the fledgling Socialist Party, or working odd jobs to supplement his $25-a-week salary. With a cause to fight and a family to support, there was no time for lounging.

Even as he sat alone on that courthouse bench, 35-year-old Carl Sandburg cut an impressive figure. Sturdy and erect, he gave the impression of being taller than he actually was. His large hands were folded in his lap, and a shock of black hair fell over his forehead. High cheekbones and ruddy skin led one acquaintance to remark that he looked like a Sioux brave. Behind the strong, imposing features, however, his hazel eyes had a wistful, faraway look. As his mind wandered, the corners of his mouth curled slowly into a grin. He drew out his notepad and scrawled a short poem:

Fog

*The fog comes
on little cat feet.*

*It sits looking
over harbor and city
on silent haunches
and then moves on.*

At the same time that he was writing tough-minded editorials on social injustice, Sandburg was quietly, in spare moments and the late hours of the night, developing a more lyrical style as a poet. His fascination with the language went back to his early youth on the Illinois prairie, where people spoke in earthy metaphors and colorful idioms. He had learned to hear poetry in everyday conversation, see harmonies in a cornfield or railroad yard. Now he was reading Japanese "haiku"—short, unrhymed poems that create simple images of nature—and experimenting with his own "free-verse" style. Ideas came to him everywhere—in his office, on a street corner, or in a trolley car. "Whenever an idea for a poem hit me," he later said, "I put it down in pencil, then worked it over at my leisure."

"Fog" was one poem he did not have to work over. It was short and simple, yet it created a vivid and lasting image. Of the more than nine hundred poems that Sandburg went on to publish in his long and celebrated career, "Fog" is perhaps the most quoted. And although it is only twenty-two words long, it says as much about Sandburg himself as any biographer could write in a thousand pages. In it there is the peacefulness, simplicity of expression, and insight into common experience that made Sandburg one of the most loved and widely read American poets of the twentieth century. At the same time it creates a vague feeling of restlessness, an urgency to move on, a yearning for the new—a spirit that Carl Sandburg demonstrated throughout his life. It is at once a meditation on nature and a declaration of freedom.

Twenty-five years later, renowned as a prose author as well as a poet, Sandburg undertook the most ambitious project of his career. Although in 1928 he was best known for his five books of poems, he had also produced two volumes of children's stories, a collection of folk songs, and a two-volume biography of Abraham Lincoln. The 1926 publication of *Abraham Lincoln: The Prairie Years* had brought the praise of critics, a multitude of honors and awards, and the financial security to leave newspaper work for good. But *The Prairie Years* was really only half a biography, ending before Lincoln's inauguration in 1861. Still to be written was the portrait of Lincoln as Civil War president. It was a massive undertaking that would take more than ten years of painstaking effort. Before it was finished, the sixteenth president of the United States had become a flesh-and-blood person to him, a companion whose death he would weep.

With the money he had earned from *The Prairie Years,* Sandburg built a large frame house atop a row of dunes on the eastern shore of Lake Michigan. It proved an ideal place to work, and it was there that Carl recreated the Lincoln presidency. He set up an office in the third-floor attic, furnishing it with a wood-burning stove, a cot, bookcases, filing cabinets, and a wooden crate for his typewriter. He liked to think that if General Grant could lead the Union war effort from a cracker box, then Carl Sandburg could work from one, too. He spent hours reading, writing, cataloguing information, rewriting, and doing more research. It wasn't long before books, documents, letters, and manuscript pages were piled ceiling-high.

Before getting started in the morning, Carl made it a habit to take a long walk on the beach. It was a chance to collect his thoughts and plan his work for the day. Neighbors on the bluff behind the beach got used to seeing a white-haired figure ambling slowly along the water's edge. They knew who he was, of course, and they could guess what he was thinking about. The gag was too good to resist.

As the story goes, a tall, lean actor was hired from Chicago and outfitted with a stovepipe hat, black beard, and long-tailed coat. The next morning, Lincoln's look-alike waited at the far end of the beach, while the pranksters settled atop the cliffs to watch the fun. When the floppy-haired writer came into view, a signal was given, and the actor began his long strides down the beach. It was timed so that the two would converge directly below the spectators' perch. As the group watched from above, Sandburg looked preoccupied as usual, his eyes fixed on the ground, his feet dragging in the sand. As the two figures drew abreast, "Lincoln" stopped to tip his hat. Sandburg looked up briefly and continued walking.

When the actor reached the other end of the beach, he pulled off his hat and beard and scrambled to the top of the bluffs.

"What happened? What did he do?" asked the disappointed practical jokers.

"Nothing," said the actor. "He looked up and kept walking."

"Did he say anything?"

"Yes, as a matter of fact he did."

"Well, what did he say? What did he say?"

"He said, 'Good morning, Mr. President.' "

Settling onto a stool at center stage, the silver-haired folksinger rolled up his sleeves, brushed an unruly lock from his eyes, and rested his "gittar" on one knee. Softly tuning each string, he greeted the audience and announced his first song, an old hobo ditty called "Wanderin'." His thick fingers labored heavily on the strings, and his hollow baritone echoed to the back row without benefit of a microphone.

> *My daddy is an engineer,*
> *My brother drives a hack,*
> *My sister takes in washin'*
> *An' the baby balls the jack,*
> *An' it looks like*
> *I'm never gonna cease my wanderin'.*
>
> *I been a-wanderin'*
> *Early and late*
> *New York City*
> *To the Golden Gate,*
> *An' it looks like*
> *I'm never gonna cease my wanderin'.*
>
> *Been a-workin' in the army*
> *Workin' on a farm,*
> *All I got to show for it*
> *Is the muscle in my arm,*
> *An' it looks like*
> *I'm never gonna cease my wanderin'.*

Carl Sandburg was not a trained musician, or even a very good one, but he loved old folk songs and delighted in performing them. When he needed a break from his work on Lincoln, he went on tour as an entertainer and lecturer, charming audiences with his wit, wisdom, and plain rendering of American ballads. Since his early days in newspapers, Sandburg had earned extra money by giving talks on subjects ranging from the labor movement to the poetry of Walt Whitman. Gradually he added some of his own poems to the program, and in 1920, during an engagement at Cornell College in Mount Vernon, Iowa, he brought out his guitar. "I will now sing a few folk songs that somehow tie into the folk quality I have tried to get into my verse," he said. "They are all authentic songs people have sung for years. If you don't care for them and want to leave, it will be all right with me. I'll be doing what I'd be doing if I were at home anyway."

Sandburg was partial to hobo songs because he had been a " 'bo" himself. Longing to see the world outside his small hometown of Galesburg, Illinois, he had hopped a freight train and set out on a youthful adventure across the Midwest. For four months on his first trip and later over a period of two years, he rode the trains, worked odd jobs, and explored new places. In boxcars and around campfires, he practiced the banjo and learned the songs of miners, cowboys, farm hands, gamblers, drinkers, jilted lovers, ex-convicts, railwaymen, and former slaves. He wrote down whatever he heard and later published the music and lyrics in a book called *The American Songbag* (1927).

"There is a human stir throughout the book, with the heights and depths to be found in Shakespeare," wrote Sandburg in the introduction. "A wide human procession

As an entertainer, Carl Sandburg brought to his performances the same love and appreciation that characterized his poetry.

marches through these pages. . . . Music and the human voice command this parade of melodies. They speak, murmur, cry, yell, laugh, pray."

Everything that Sandburg did in life, all that he wrote and all that he sang, had this same "human stir." On the written page and the music-hall stage, he was the voice of ordinary men and women—farmers, factory workers, shop girls, and soldiers. These were the people he knew best and cared about most. He was of their stock and of their spirit. In dress, in speech, and in point of view he was always—and proudly so—one of "the people." His art reflected his personality—simple, rough-hewn, and free of pretense. His life and his life's work were all of a kind, always in close harmony.

Carl Sandburg once said of himself: "Among the biographers, I am a first-rate poet. And among the poets, a good biographer; among singers, I'm a good collector of songs, and among song collectors a good judge of pipes."

Ernest Hemingway, no pushover when it came to judging fellow writers, was among the many who gave him more credit than that. In 1954, when Hemingway received the Nobel Prize for Literature, the first thing he told reporters was that there was another writer more deserving: Carl Sandburg. Although Sandburg never did win the Nobel, he was showered with prizes, awards, medals, citations, and honorary degrees throughout his career. He won the Pulitzer Prize twice—in 1940 for *Abraham Lincoln: The War Years* and in 1950 for his *Complete Poems.* He delivered a special address before the U.S. Congress and was decorated by the king of Sweden. His seventy-fifth birthday—January 6, 1953—was declared "Carl Sandburg Day" in Chicago. Schools were named after him from San Bruno, California, to Rockville, Maryland. Beyond all the formal recognition, Sandburg was also one of the most popular and admired figures of his time. His books were read by millions; his voice was heard in music halls from coast to coast; and his face—high cheekbones, deep lines, and white locks hanging over one eye—was recognized around the world.

Private and self-effacing, Sandburg was not entirely comfortable with his celebrity status. It was not his nature to be distracted by public adoration, as deep and genuine as it was. There was always too much to be done, too much more to learn. "A celebrity," he once said, "is a fellow who eats celery with celerity." (Dryly translated: fame is just a word, and a pretty meaningless one, at that.)

Poet, biographer, journalist, children's writer, novelist, folklorist, and screenwriter, Sandburg was a literary jack-of-all-trades. But because he tried so many different kinds of writing, and because he was never a "profound" or "fancy" writer, he was not always taken seriously. Despite its mass appeal, his poetry was frequently criticized for its simplicity, colloquialism, and "cracker-barrel" philosophy. While some historians praised his Lincoln work as the greatest biography ever written by an American, others called it whimsical and overly poetic. His lone novel, *Remembrance Rock* (1948), was dismissed by one critic as being unworthy of even a review.

Since his death in 1967, Sandburg has had a mixed reputation: he is still widely read, especially in schools, but he is largely ignored in the literary community. Sandburg probably would not have minded much. His poems are most often criticized for the very qualities he valued most. They lack polish and sophistication, it is said. They are simple and informal. They ask too many questions, answer too few. They lack discipline and subtlety. They are homespun and uneducated. They are the work, said the poet Ezra Pound, of "a lumberjack who taught himself everything he knows."

Pound happened to be wrong on both counts. With all the odd jobs that Carl had before becoming a writer—milkman, shoe-shine boy, fireman, salesman, farm hand, house painter, and soldier—he never did try his hand at lumberjacking. As for education, Sandburg left school after the eighth grade but did attend college. There he worked closely under a noted scholar, Professor Philip Green Wright, and read the classics in literature, politics, religion, and philosophy. The only things that kept him from graduating were a few credits and a yearning to travel.

—9—

Indeed Sandburg's education did not end in the classroom. "All my life I have been trying to learn to read, to see and hear, and to write," he declared in the preface to his *Complete Poems.* His real "school" was the world outside; his lifelong teacher was personal experience. Like other great Midwestern writers of his generation—Hemingway, Theodore Dreiser, Sinclair Lewis, and Sherwood Anderson—Sandburg was a realist. He wrote of ordinary things, of the here and now, of real people and real places. He was independent-minded and free-spirited. He was indifferent to trends and fashions, stubbornly individualistic in everything he did and wrote. There was little deviation in his purpose, and there are no distinct "periods" in his poetry or prose. His life's work is a celebration of industrial and agricultural America—their language, folklore, history, and people. Like Abraham Lincoln, also born of the prairie, Sandburg believed deeply in the ideals of his nation and the enduring strength of its citizens. In his book-length poem *The People, Yes* (1936) he wrote:

> *The people will live on.*
> *The learning and blundering people will live on.*
> *They will be tricked and sold and again sold*
> *And go back to the nourishing earth for rootholds,*
> *The people so peculiar in renewal and comeback,*
> *You can't laugh off their capacity to take it.*

And in his prologue to "The Family of Man," a 1955 photographic exhibition by his brother-in-law and close friend, Edward Steichen, he wrote:

> *In a seething of saints and sinners, winners or losers, in a womb of superstition, faith, genius, crime, sacrifice, here is the People, the one and only source of armies, navies, work-gangs, the living flowing breath of the history of nations, ever lighted by the reality or illusion of hope. Hope is a sustaining human gift.*

The final reputation of any writer is difficult to predict. So much depends on history and circumstance, tastes and trends. In the case of a very few, however, the contributions are unmistakable. While Carl Sandburg may never be regarded on the same level as Shakespeare, Whitman, or even Robert Frost, he was the mouthpiece for an entire generation of Americans. Few writers have ever touched so many people, so closely. While he may not have been so "poetic" or so "profound" as some others, his unique free-verse style—which he called "folksay"—did a great deal to revive American poetry in the early twentieth century.

As for the writing itself, several of his works still stand as important literary creations. His six-volume study of Abraham Lincoln remains the longest, most thorough, and most lyrical biography in American literature. A handful of poems— "Fog," "Chicago," parts of "The People, Yes," and others— are considered classics. The autobiography of his youth, *Always the Young Strangers* (1953), has endured as a vivid recreation of small-town America before the turn of the century. Finally, his folksong collections have been an invaluable contribution to the national lore.

The legacy of Carl Sandburg was summarized in a eulogy by President Lyndon Johnson in July 1967:

> There is no end to the legacy he leaves us. Carl Sandburg was more than the voice of America, more than the poet of its strength and genius. He was America. We knew and cherished him as the bard of democracy, the echo of the people, our conscience, and chronicler of truth and beauty and purpose.

BOY OF THE PRAIRIE

2

I was born on the prairie and the milk of its wheat,
the red of its clover, the eyes of its women, gave
me a song and a slogan. . . .
O prairie mother, I am one of your boys.

"Prairie"

Galesburg, Illinois, in the late 1800s was a small prairie town in the northwestern part of the state, population 15,000. It had been founded a generation earlier by settlers from New England and upper New York State. Until the coming of the railroads, life in Galesburg was dominated by the Presbyterian and Congregationalist churches, Republican politics, and the town's three colleges. Knox College, Lombard College, and Brown's Business College together earned Galesburg the nicknames "College City" and "Athens of the Corn Belt." But when the Santa Fe Railroad made Galesburg a stop along its route to Chicago, and when the Chicago, Burlington, and Quincy Railroad (C.B.&Q.) built shops in the town, the character of Galesburg changed markedly. The opportunities for employment attracted thousands of immigrants, mostly Swedish Lutherans and Irish Catholics. New accents were heard in the streets. New churches went up. It was, as its most famous son described it, "a piece of the American Republic."

THE SANDBURGS

"I don't know who my ancestors were but we've been descending for a long time," quipped Carl Sandburg in his autobiography, *Always the Young Strangers.* His mother and father were both Swedish immigrants who met and married in America. They spoke Swedish at home and followed many of their native customs, but they told their children little about life in the Old Country. Many years later, in an emotional visit to the "homeland," Carl saw firsthand how his parents—and their parents—had grown up. The countryside reminded him of Illinois.

Carl's father was born August Danielsson in the village of Asbo. The family was poor and lived as peasants. In 1856, when Alfred was ten, the Danielssons boarded a sailing vessel as steerage passengers and set out for America with dreams of greater opportunity. Alfred's parents died in an epidemic shortly after arriving, and the boy was on his own. A cousin wrote him that there were plenty of jobs in an Illinois town called Galesburg, and Danielsson worked his way west on a railroad gang. Because there were so many other Swedes in the crew whose names ended in "-son," he decided to choose a new name for himself: Sandburg.

Carl's mother, Clara Mathilda Andersdotter, was born and reared in the town of Appuna, not far from Asbo. When Clara was six, her mother died and her father remarried. Clara did not get along well with her stepmother and in 1872, at age twenty-two, left for the United States. She landed as a hotel chambermaid in the town of Bushnell, Illinois, where she met August Sandburg, passing through on the railroad gang. The couple was married in August 1874 and settled in Galesburg.

August Sandburg had straight black hair, "eyes rather deep-set in the bone, and the skin crinkled with his smile or laugh. He was somewhat below medium height . . . , well muscled, the skin of his chest showing a pale white against the grime when his collar was turned down." He swung a hammer at the C.B.&Q. blacksmith shop from seven in the morning until six at night, for fourteen cents an hour. It took him fifteen minutes every evening, Carl remembered, to wash the soot and grime from his hands, face, and neck. August Sandburg never learned to write and signed his name with an "X." He could read Swedish, however, and when he wasn't immersed in the Bible he enjoyed the weekly *Hemlandet* ("Homeland") from Chicago. He was a quiet, devout man who worked hard, showed little emotion, and went to church regularly.

Clara Sandburg was fair and had softer features than August, her hair "the color of oat straw just before the sun tans it—eyes light-blue, the skin white as fresh linen by candlelight, the mouth for smiling." She was a strong, patient woman who kept a modestly comfortable household on August's meager earnings. She woke at six every morning to cook breakfast, then make the beds, wash and mend clothes, shop for groceries, and prepare dinner.

Clara and August Sandburg had their first child, Mary, in 1875. Over the next eighteen years, Clara gave birth to six more: Carl, Martin, Emil, Esther, Fred, and Martha. Clara loved the children more openly than August, but both parents kept a close guiding hand. Honesty, integrity, the work ethic, and a love for the land were carefully nurtured in each child. The Sandburg family was Lutheran in faith, Republican in politics, and old-fashioned in values.

Carl Sandburg was born on a cornhusk mattress in a three-room cottage on East Third Street, January 6, 1878. He was baptized Carl August Sandburg, but the name "Charlie August" was entered in the family Bible. In the first year of grade school he began signing his name "Charles A. Sandburg," thinking it sounded more American than "Carl." His father had trouble pronouncing "ch" and called him "Sharley." His brothers and sisters took to calling him "Cully," a nickname that stuck all the way through college.

Baby Carl was delivered by a midwife and put in a cradle that August had built himself. Within two days of giving birth, Clara was back on her feet cutting out diapers from flour sacks. Carl's first words were Swedish: *mor* (mother), *far* (father), and *mjolk* (milk).

At the age of three, Mary later told him, he "ran away" from home; after a frantic search, his father found him several blocks away. But Carl remembered nothing of that incident, nor anything else of the tiny cottage on Third Street. From their next house, on South Street, Cully did remember helping his father in the garden. "I can never forget," he wrote many years later, "the feel of potatoes and carrots as my fingers brushed the loam off them and I threw them into the baskets."

The Sandburgs had an old mare named Dolly, whom they hitched to a wagon for rides on the prairie. On Sundays after church they often visited the Kranses, relatives who lived on a thirty-acre farm a few miles away. The outings were a source of wonder and joy for young Carl. He drank milk from the cows he saw give it, ate eggs from the hens he saw lay them, and frolicked in the fields and pastures with little Charlie Krans. Riding home under the stars, he fell asleep exhausted in the back of the wagon.

Galesburg and the Sandburg family weathered some hard times during Carl's youth. August worked only four hours a day when things were bad, bringing home a mere fourteen dollars a month. A new pair of shoes was the grandest of luxuries. Butter was a rare item on the table; cabbage or boiled herring, always with potatoes, was dinner. Despite all the hardship, Clara and August managed to save some money and buy a spacious, ten-room house at 622-24 East Berrien Street. It was on a large lot with maple trees, gooseberry bushes, and a henhouse. August was able to rent out four rooms to help make his payments, and life got easier for the Sandburgs. It was in the house on Berrien Street that young Carl graduated "from dresses to short pants to long pants, from a babbler with bibs to a grown man."

WORK AND PLAY

On the dusty streets and vacant lots of Galesburg, Cully Sandburg enjoyed a carefree childhood typical of a small Midwestern town in the 1880s. Despite the financial problems at home, he always remembered his youth as totally without unpleasantness. After school and before dinner, he played games in the street—mumblety-peg, two-old-cat, and duck on a rock—with his brother Martin and other children in the neighborhood. When he got a little older, he went swimming in the pond and started playing sports.

Baseball was his favorite. His dream was to become a big-leaguer, and sometimes he played from eight in the morning until it was too dark to see the ball. He knew the names of all the professional stars and memorized their statistics from the newspaper. Indeed, baseball would become a lifelong passion. Sandburg had hundreds of stories about the game, and he often brought it up to make a serious point. In the preface to his *Complete Poems,* for example, he drew the following analogy to a poet's intuition:

> *Interviewing Babe Ruth in 1928 for the Chicago* Daily News, *I put it to him, "People come and ask what's your secret for hitting home runs—that so?" "Yes," said the Babe, "and all I can tell 'em is I pick a good one and sock it."*

And he made a similar point in the poem "Style":

> *Style—go ahead talking about style.*
> *You can tell where a man gets his style just*
> *   as you can tell where Pavlova got her legs*
> *   or Ty Cobb his batting eye.*

The county fair was another of Sandburg's warm childhood memories. Once a year, he and a group of friends made the five-mile hike to the town of Knoxville, where the fair was held. There they took in all the sights, sounds, and smells of rural life in the Midwest. They marveled at the prizewinning livestock and stared at the tall, leather-skinned farmers. One year Cully and his friends each paid a nickel to hear the Edison Talking Phonograph, a wondrous new invention that brought sounds from faraway places. The animals, the people, the machines, and the haystack rides all made a deep, lasting impression on young Sandburg.

But life for Cully was not all street games, baseball, and

county fairs. Not the least of his other activities were chores around the house. One of his first jobs was to break up chunks of coal to fit in the heating stove. The stove was located in the kitchen and heated only a small portion of the house. On cold winter nights, Cully and Martin would warm themselves in front of the stove, then run upstairs to their third-floor garret and jump into bed. Later the family acquired a more modern appliance, with an isinglass (mica) door and an ashpan at the bottom. It was Cully's job to carry out the ashpan and empty it on a pile behind the potato patch.

A chore that Sandburg remembered doing thousands of times was pumping fresh water in the backyard and lugging the full pails back to the house. The pump had a wooden handle, and sometimes it was all the boy could do to get it to work. In the summer, when the pump needed priming, he would pour water into the conveyor. In the winter, when it froze, he would thaw it out with a bucket of hot water. He yelled at it, swore at it, apologized to it, and was back again later in the day to pump some more. "Its two-way stretch," one biographer has noted, "had a rhythm similar to some lines of the Sandburg poetry."

By the time he was ten, Charlie was taking odd jobs—collecting bottles, rags, and iron scraps—to bring in money for the family. He got his first regular paid job at age eleven, opening up a real estate office every morning before school. For twenty-five cents a week he arrived at the office at 7:45, unlocked the doors, cleaned the spittoons, and swept the floor from end to end.

Like so many other boys his age, Cully also delivered newspapers. He reported to the *Republican-Register* every day after school, folded his sixty newspapers, and set off on his two-mile route. In making his rounds, young Sandburg began to notice differences in how people lived. Some had vast, forbidding residences while others had humble, friendlier homes with modest front yards and rickety wooden porches. One of Charlie's customers was the Republican Party boss for Knox County, a fat old man who trudged to his front gate and greedily swiped the newspaper from the boy's hand. It was the one delivery Cully hated most.

For delivering the *Republican-Register,* Charlie got a free copy of the paper and a shiny silver dollar every week. Looking to earn more money, he gave up his job at the real estate office to deliver the morning papers from Chicago. This meant walking to the train station before dawn, grabbing the papers off the mail car, and loading up his wagon with as many as it could hold. He sold each copy for a nickel and kept a penny for himself. Between the two delivery routes, he sometimes earned twelve dollars in a month. The work also gave him a keen insight into the ways of business and sparked an abiding interest in the newspaper field.

It was at the Fourth and Seventh Ward grammar schools that Cully Sandburg learned the alphabet and began to read. His first lesson book had a silly story about a women's tea party, and the Bible was the only book in the Sandburg household. But Charlie was strangely excited by the world of books. With the encouragement of his sixth-grade teacher, Miss Goldquist, he took out a card from the public library and became an avid reader. When Clara Sandburg paid seventy-five cents to a door-to-door salesman for the one-volume *Cyclopaedia of Important Facts of the World,* Charlie was overjoyed. He hugged it close to his chest and lost himself in it for days.

Geography was Charlie's favorite subject in school, and though he read *Tom Sawyer* and *Huckleberry Finn* by the popular Mark Twain, he much preferred James Otis's *Toby Tyler: or, Ten Weeks with a Circus* and Champlin's *Young Folks' Cyclopaedia of Persons and Places.* Most of all he liked history books and biographies of Revolutionary War generals. Memorable among these were *Washington and His Generals* and *Napoleon and His Marshals,* both by J. T. Headley. His very favorite books were all by Charles Carleton Coffin: *The Boys of '76,* which he read three or four times and, he later wrote, "made me feel I could have been a boy in the days of George Washington"; *Old Times in the Colonies;* and *The Story of Liberty.* Coffin's book about the Civil War, however, *The Boys of '61,* struck the young reader as "dry and stupid," even though he was deeply interested in the subject.

HISTORY, POLITICS, AND
BLOOD IN THE STREETS

The Civil War was a topic still very much alive in Galesburg. The town had been against slavery from the very time it was settled; no one could join any of its churches unless he favored abolition. Before and during the war, Galesburg was an important station in the "underground railroad"; runaway slaves were hidden in the steeple of the Old First Church and aided in their escape to Canada. Less than thirty years after the Confederate surrender, veterans from both sides were still living in town, recounting their adventures at Gettysburg, Antietam, and Bull Run. One such man, a carpenter named Joe Elser, rented a room in the Sandburgs' house and spent hours with the children reenacting battles and describing his life as a Union soldier.

Cully's interest in "The War" had first been aroused in July 1885, at age seven, when a funeral was held in Galesburg for the Union general and President of the United States, Ulysses S. Grant. The solemn parade down Main Street—complete with marching band, fife-and-drum corps, horses, cannons, and flags—made young Sandburg want to learn more about the war, the freeing of the slaves, and what it was like to be president.

While Grant's funeral remained vivid in Sandburg's memory, he had an even earlier recollection of crowds in the streets of Galesburg. This was in October 1884, when a torchlight rally was held for Republican presidential candidate James G. Blaine. That night the brass band and the beat of drums were drowned out by shouting. "Blaine! Blaine! James G. Blaine!" yelled half the mob. "Hurray for Cleveland! Grover Cleveland for President!" came the voice of Democrats on behalf of their candidate. August Sandburg favored Blaine, though he would not join with some others in calling for a rope to hang Cleveland. Six-year-old Cully Sandburg also thought of himself as a Republican and wondered if someday he, too; might march with a "flambeau."

Most unforgettable of all was a strike in 1888 by engineers of the Chicago, Burlington & Quincy Railroad. The engineers' slogan was "Come Boys and Quit Railroading," a take-off on the abbreviation C.B.&Q. This time there was fighting in the streets, even shooting. On their way to school, Charlie and the other boys saw the spot where an engineer had been killed, his blood turned dry on the wooden sidewalk. There was angry talk about "scabs," men willing to work in place of the strikers. August refused to take any part in the action for fear of losing his job. Young Carl was against the railroad and for the workers, though he was not really sure why. What he did begin to see clearly were the greed, injustice, violence—and courage—of which some men were capable. The union man, the scab, and the industrialist would someday find a place—alongside the farmer, the blacksmith, the Union soldier, the children playing, and even the animals—in Sandburg's portrait of life in the Midwest.

SCRAPS
AND PIECES

3

In 1891, at the age of thirteen, Charlie Sandburg was confirmed in the Elim Lutheran Chapel and graduated from the Churchill Grammar School. He had never liked church very much, but he always loved school. Unfortunately his parents could afford to support only one student, and Mary was the eldest. So, after the eighth grade, Cully went to work full-time to help buy books and clothes for his sister. His childhood had come to an end, but his education, even if it was no longer in the classroom, continued:

> In those years as a boy in that prairie town I got education in scraps and pieces of many kinds, not knowing that they were part of my education. I met people in Galesburg who were puzzling to me, and later when I read Shakespeare I found those same people were puzzling him. I met little wonders of many kinds among animals and plants that never lost their wonder for me, and I found later that these same wonders had a deep interest for Emerson, Thoreau, and Walt Whitman. I met superstitions, folk tales, and folklore while I was a young spalpeen, 'a broth of a boy,' long before I read books about them. All had their part, small or large, in the education I got outside of books and schools.

MUSIC AND SONG

The first musical instrument Carl Sandburg ever played was a "willow whistle," a small reed that produced a single shrill

Cully Sandburg at the time
of his graduation from
Churchill Grammar School in 1891

note when blown just right. Next came a comb and tissue paper, followed by a dime-store kazoo, a tin fife, a wooden flageolet (like a recorder), and an ocarina. His first stringed instrument was a cigar-box banjo, which he made himself. Finally, when he started to earn some money of his own, he bought a two-dollar used banjo from Mr. Gumbiner's pawn shop. Cully's friend Willis Calkins taught him a few chords, and Mrs. Schwartz on Ferris Street gave him three lessons for twenty-five cents apiece.

Young Charlie Sandburg grew up in an environment rich in music and song. His father played old Swedish folk songs on the accordion, and Mary accompanied on a small foot-pedal organ. After dinner, when schoolwork and chores were done, the family would gather in the front parlor to sing and dance. When he got a little older, Cully would meet Willis and some other friends in front of the local cigar store to harmonize their favorite ballads and folk songs. Passers-by would stop to hear their gay renditions of "Suwannee River," "Carry Me Back to Old Virginny," and other popular tunes.

MILK SLINGER,
ICE CUTTER, BOOTBLACK

Though later in life Sandburg would be paid for performing on stage, music now was only a way to relax between jobs or to unwind at the end of a workday. Perhaps no American youth has ever held the variety of jobs that Cully Sandburg did between the ages of thirteen and nineteen. Each one taught him new things about himself, about other people, and about the world around him.

Charlie's first full-time job after leaving school was delivering milk for a sour-tempered dairyman named George Burton. At six in the morning, seven days a week, Sandburg walked the two miles to Burton's dairy barn and filled two large cans to the brim. Lugging the milk cans through town, he stopped to fill the bottles and pails at each house along the route.

In October 1892, not long after he started the job, Charlie came down with a sore throat and had to miss a few days of work. Burton was suspicious, thinking the boy was shirking his responsibility; Charlie knew he could not work for the man much longer. The next week, Charlie's brothers Martin, Emil, and Fred also came down with sore throats. Martin was back on his feet within four days, but Emil, just turning seven, and Freddie, only two, got sicker and sicker. A doctor was called in and made a frightening diagnosis: diphtheria. There was nothing for the family to do but hope. On the third day, a half-hour apart, the two boys stopped breathing. Charlie felt the loss very deeply, especially for Emil, more of a companion to him than the infant Fred. For two nights, Charlie and Mart cried in their beds, but at the funeral they fought back the tears.

During the week of his brothers' illness and death, Charlie missed only another two days of work, even though the Sandburg house had been put under quarantine. George Burton was more upset about the boy's absence than about his family tragedy and did not even offer condolences. Charlie quit. Rather than hating Mr. Burton, he left feeling sorry for the lack of compassion or joy in the man's own life.

Over the next several years, young Sandburg held a hodgepodge of jobs in and around Galesburg. He was a tinsmith's assistant, pharmacist's chore boy, bottle washer, stagehand, fruit vendor, horse sponger, bootblack, ice cutter, and milkman again (though not for George Burton). Ice cutting, bootblacking, and "milk slinging," in particular, provided experiences that he would value for the rest of his life.

The most physically demanding work Sandburg ever did was for the Glenwood Ice Company one January. For the two-week ice harvest on Lake George, Charlie was part of a gang that labored from seven at night until six in the morning, with an hour off at midnight. Huge blocks of ice were broken off the lake surface, floated to the icehouse, cut into blocks, and stored in sawdust until summer. During his first week on the job, Charlie worked as a "floater," propelling great rafts of ice to the icehouse with a long pole. Though he went home tired every morning, he enjoyed the crisp night air and invigorating outdoor work. Floating across the water, he would gaze at the star-filled sky and follow the rotation of the constellations. "I did my wondering about that spread of changing stars," he later wrote, "and how little any one of us is standing looking up at it."

His second week, however, proved considerably more arduous and with none of the pleasures of the outdoors. Taken off as a floater, he was put inside the icehouse and handed a pair of tongs to unload the blocks and stack them in rows. Charlie only weighed about 115 pounds, and many of the ice cakes were heavier than he was. Clamping the tongs into the thick blocks, hauling them twenty or thirty feet, and standing them upright strained every muscle in his body. He went to bed aching from head to heels, and on his third night he resolved to quit. The foreman found him daydreaming and told him to get to work. "Better slide into it, Sandburg," said the foreman, "there's only a few more days on this job." That was all Cully needed. He slept better, his muscles loosened, and he saw through his fortnight's commitment. The lesson he learned was to keep his work in perspective, pace himself, and not give up before a task was finished.

The job Sandburg later regarded as his most worthwhile in Galesburg was shining shoes and sweeping floors in a downtown barbershop. Despite the variety and interest of his work experience so far, Charlie had felt that he really wasn't getting anywhere. He wanted to learn a trade, but there were no opportunities with any of the local plumbers, machinists, or carpenters. When a job opened up at Humphrey's Barbershop, he jumped at the chance. There was no future in bootblacking, he realized, but perhaps he could learn barbering and someday open a shop of his own. In the meantime, Mr. Humphrey would pay him three dollars a week in addition to his shoeshine money and tips.

Humphrey's was located in the basement of the Union

Hotel building, directly below a bank, and it attracted many of the influential people who came to town. One memorable morning, before a funeral for a local politician, Cully Sandburg shined the shoes of four senators, eight congressmen, and four army majors. When things were slow in the shop, the boy especially enjoyed scouting the hotel lobby for confidence men, swindlers, and gamblers whose pictures he had seen in the *Police Gazette*. As the weeks passed, however, young Sandburg came to realize that the most interesting people of all were ordinary men from around town. Their jokes were the funniest, their stories the most entertaining, their arguments the loudest, and their language the most colorful. Their simple expressions, homely metaphors, platitudes, and proverbs seemed to say so much more than the fancy language of senators and congressmen. During his six months at Humphrey's, young Sandburg had a thorough education in the history, idioms, folklore, and values of the American heartland—just by listening to people talk. As for barbering, Charlie gradually realized he wasn't "cut out" for it and left the shop in the spring of 1895.

At the age of seventeen, Charlie went back to milk slinging, this time for a dairyman named Samuel Kossuth Barlow. Before going into the milk business, Barlow had been a farmer and a fiddler at country dances. Unlike George Burton, he was a pleasant, friendly man who thought highly of his young helper. During their long hours on the milk wagon, Sam and Cully talked about everything from politics to religion to women. They were together nearly every day for a year and a half and stayed close friends until Barlow's death years later.

"MORAL LIGHTS" AND RADICAL POLITICS

Every morning on the way to Barlow's dairy barn, Charlie passed through the Knox College campus and lingered a moment in front of a red-brick building called the Old Main. On the north face of Old Main, a bronze plaque had been put up to commemorate the most famous event in Galesburg's history. On October 7, 1858, only twenty years before Sandburg was born, a crowd of twenty thousand had stood in a cold wind to hear the fifth in a series of debates between senatorial opponents Abraham Lincoln and Stephen A. Douglas. It was in these debates that Lincoln committed his career to the abolition of slavery and won national recognition as a possible candidate for the White House. Words he spoke that day were memorialized on the bronze plaque, and Cully Sandburg learned them by heart: "He is blowing out the moral lights around us, when he contends that whoever wants slaves has a right to hold them."

Galesburg before the turn of the century still remembered Abraham Lincoln as a live presence, his voice still clear, his handshake still warm. There were men around town who had met him as a young politician and recounted the stories he had told them. "Yes, sir," they would say proudly, "I once met Abe Lincoln under that maple tree and he told me the story about . . ." An old Knox professor once had an office next to Lincoln's at the statehouse and was said to be the last man to shake his hand before he boarded the train to Washington. Fact had given way to fancy over the years, but Galesburg still thought of Honest Abe as one of its own. For Cully Sandburg, the rich history and mythology surrounding the figure of Abraham Lincoln planted the seeds of a lifelong fascination.

Another public figure whom young Sandburg deeply admired was Governor John P. Altgeld. Charlie first heard Altgeld speak at the Galesburg Opera House in 1892, when the controversial Democrat was running for office. A few months after being elected, Governor Altgeld decided to pardon the three surviving anarchists who had been convicted of killing seven policemen in Chicago's Haymarket Square labor riots of 1886. Having carefully reviewed the case, Altgeld concluded that there had been insufficient evidence to convict the men and that they had been the victims of political prejudice. His decision aroused a storm of protest and ultimately spelled the end of his career in politics. Charlie Sandburg, for one, had taken the time to read Altgeld's long statement, and he found it sober and just. It was an important awakening in Sandburg's life, and John Altgeld was someone he always pointed to as a model of courage, wisdom, and moral strength.

Though he did not have the privilege of going to school, Cully was reading more books and developing a broader social awareness than most of his peers still in the classroom. Riding a milk wagon or sitting up at night, he read speeches, poems, novels, almanacs, and anything else he could get his hands on. Among the writings that left the deepest impression were those by the liberal politician and orator William Jennings Bryan. In 1894, after hearing one of Bryan's impassioned and eloquent speeches in person, Charlie announced—to his father's horror—that he would become a Democrat. Though he later recognized that Bryan was more wind than wisdom, sixteen-year-old Carl Sandburg regarded him as "the Man of the People who spoke for the right."

Also influential in the development of Sandburg's radical political opinions was a boyhood chum named John Sjodin. The son of a journeyman tailor and political activist from Chicago, John could talk for hours about the oppression of workers, the power of "big business," and the futility of both the Republican and Democratic parties. The time would come, he proclaimed, when farmers and factory workers would organize and wrest power from the wealthy oppressors. Socialism would have its day, and soon.

Charlie began to spend more and more time at Knox College, attending debates, lectures, club meetings, poetry readings, concerts, and graduation exercises in the spring. One of his most memorable events was a special celebration on October 7, 1896, to mark the thirty-eighth anniversary of the Lincoln-Douglas debate. The featured guest was Chauncey M. Depew, president of the New York Central Railroad, a leader of Lincoln's campaign in 1864, and one of the most popular after-dinner speakers in the country. Of greater interest to Cully Sandburg, however, was the scheduled appearance by Robert Todd Lincoln, son of the Great Emancipator. Robert Todd Lincoln had served as Secretary of War under Presidents Garfield and Arthur, and now worked as an attorney for the Pullman Company in Chicago. Charlie wondered what it was like to be the son of Abraham Lincoln, what life was like in the White House, and what personal memories Robert Todd had of his father. But the speech was a disappointment. It was very short and gave young Sandburg little to think about.

It was about this time also that Cully got involved with a small "gang" called the Dirty Dozen. The Dirty Dozen did not get into fights or break the law; they were not that kind of gang. They had their fun by pulling pranks and practical jokes around Galesburg, and they went to jail only once. That was for swimming nude in a remote mudhole outside of town. A night behind bars for skinny-dipping struck Cully as excessive punishment, and the whole incident left him with a bitter feeling toward the police and authority in general.

LOOKING TO HORIZONS

In June 1896 Charlie's father got him a free pass to Chicago on the C.B.&Q. He had heard so much about the "Windy City" from John Sjodin and had read so much about it in the newspapers he delivered. Now he would finally see it for himself. With $1.50 in his pocket and no luggage, he boarded the train on the morning of June 15. One by one, the towns of Galva, Kewanee, Mendota, and Aurora flashed past his window. Cully could hardly contain his excitement. He felt grown up and independent, ready to find out what life was really like in the big city.

The train pulled into Union Station at two in the afternoon, and for the next three days Cully explored the city from early in the morning until late at night. He slept in a shabby hotel for twenty-five cents a night and took his meals at Pittsburgh Joe's diner. The rest of the day he walked. He visited the *Daily News* building, Marshall Field's department store, the Loop, and all the other places he had heard so much about. Making his way east across the city, he came to the shore of Lake Michigan and was dazzled by the vast blue water stretching to the horizon. It was a sight he later described in a poem called "The Harbor":

> *Out from the huddled and ugly walls,*
> *I came sudden, at the city's edge,*
> *On a blue burst of lake,*
> *Long lake waves breaking under the sun*
> *On a spray-flung curve of shore . . .*

Chicago and its people would be a creative inspiration to Carl Sandburg for many years to come, and his first eye-opening visit that June planted the seed of his poetic vision. Nothing escaped him in this noisy, bustling, crowded city. He saw how the wealthy merchants and industrialists lived, and how the stockyard workers, shop clerks, and washerwomen lived. He marveled at the skyscrapers and shuddered at the slums. Perhaps it was from first-hand experience that he later wrote of "painted women under the gas lamps luring the farm boys." The great world outside had been opened up to him—like the "blue burst of lake"—and Galesburg would never be big enough again.

By the time he was eighteen, then, Cully Sandburg had come under many of the influences and developed many of the interests that would form the foundation of his entire life's work. Born on the prairie, he had grown up among simple people and learned the simple virtues of honesty, hard work, and love of the land. He had watched and listened, absorbing the language and folklore of America's heartland. Poverty and social injustice were part of the everyday life around him; politics and labor unrest had run hot in the streets of his hometown. He learned to think for himself and developed radical ideas for improving the lot of his fellow men. He read history books and the biographies of great leaders. He discovered the joys of music and poetry. He heard firsthand accounts of the Civil War, and he learned about Abraham Lincoln from men who had actually met him. Finally, he had a glimpse of life in the big city, of industrial America at work, of what lay outside the small prairie town of Galesburg.

Not long after returning from Chicago, young Sandburg made a startling declaration to his sister Mary. "I'm going away," he confided. "I'm going to be a writer. And if I can't be a writer, I'll be a hobo."

WANDERIN'

4

On a bright afternoon in June 1897 Carl Sandburg left home with his life's savings of $3.25 and the clothes on his back. He had grown to his full height of five feet, ten inches, and his frame was well-muscled with six years of hard physical labor. Broad-shouldered and verging on manhood, he set out from Galesburg with an exhilarating sense of anticipation, adventure, and uncertainty. A Santa Fe Railroad freight train pulled out of the station, and Charlie ran alongside until he came to the open doorway of a boxcar. He leaped in, climbed to his feet, and watched the countryside roll by.

Heading west, the train passed through green cornfields and small towns, crossed a long bridge over the Mississippi River, and veered south in Iowa. At Fort Madison, Sandburg jumped out as the train slowed into the station. He bought a nickel's worth of cheese and crackers, and gazed across the Mississippi as he ate. A steamboat captain offered him passage to Keokuk if he would help unload some cargo, and Charlie quickly accepted. At Keokuk he slept on a bed of newspapers, with a coat over his shoulders, near a canal. There he met a hobo who gave him a "lump" (a package of roast beef and buttered bread) and a few pointers on how to take care of himself on the road. As the two sat talking, the hobo put a hand on him in a way that made Charlie nervous. The wide-eyed young traveler took to his heels, apprehensive about the entire mission.

Realizing he would need more money to live on, Cully found an old tin can, invested in a paintbrush and some liquid asphalt, and went from house to house blacking rusty stoves.

The first day he earned seventy-five cents and two free meals. Later that week, on the Fourth of July, he landed a job waiting tables at a luncheonette. During the short time he worked there, Cully ate as much as his stomach could hold and stashed away two thick sandwiches and a few doughnuts for the road. Then it was back on a freight train, heading south to Missouri. In a place called Bean Lake, he worked on a railroad gang until he had his fill of the overbearing foreman and the steady diet of fried potatoes and pork.

Young Sandburg was away four months on that first adventure outside Illinois. He sold hot tamales on the streets of Kansas City; pitched wheat in Pawnee County, Kansas; washed dishes in Denver; chopped wood and picked apples in Nebraska; and thrived on his freedom every step of the way. There was dramatic adventure, and there was tedium. There were kind people, and there was the "shack" (railroad brakeman) who beat him up and threatened to toss him off the train if he didn't hand over twenty-five cents. There was the camaraderie of hobo "jungles," and there was the loneliness of traveling alone. At a farm in Kansas, he overheard some Swedish workers call him a "bum," and he concluded it must be true. But there was a difference between a hobo and a bum that perhaps Charlie didn't consider. A bum begs for handouts, while a hobo takes odd jobs to pay for his food and shelter. "A hobo is a travellin' man," went an old song, "but he ain't no bum, bum, bum." Charlie was no bum either, working his way across the land, making a go of things on his own initiative and his own sweat.

From the very first day of his trip, Sandburg kept a diary of all his experiences. In two small notebooks, he described his many adventures and recorded his impressions of the land and its people. He listened carefully to the way people spoke and wrote down their sayings and expressions. He played word games of his own, and he jotted down the songs he heard in boxcars, farmhouses, and hobo jungles.

In mid-October 1897 Charlie arrived back in Galesburg with fifteen dollars and a few nickels in his pocket. He was still uncertain what the future would hold for him, but he knew he had changed. "Away deep in my heart now," he later wrote, "I had hope as never before. Struggles lay ahead, I was sure, but whatever they were I would not be afraid of them."

PRIVATE SANDBURG

Resolving to learn a trade and make something of himself, Cully took a job as an apprentice to a local house painter. For nearly six months he climbed ladders, scraped old buildings, and sandpapered the walls for more experienced workers to paint fresh. He never even wielded a brush, and by the spring of 1898 he was restless again.

In February of that year Charlie heard about the sinking of the battleship *Maine* in Havana Harbor. War between the United States and Spain broke out on April 25, and the very next day twenty-year-old Cully Sandburg enlisted for two years in Company C, Sixth Infantry Regiment of the Illinois Volunteers. He was given the same dark-blue uniform and bayoneted rifle that Union soldiers had used thirty-five years before. The company drilled for ten days in Springfield, where Sandburg spent his free time visiting the state capital grounds and the grave site of Abraham Lincoln. Then it was on to Falls Church, Virginia, only a few miles outside Washington, D. C. With his one day's leave, Charlie managed to see the White House, the Capitol, Ford's Theater, and the Peterson House, where President Lincoln had died.

Finally, in July, the Illinois company boarded the freighter *Rita* and set out for Guantanamo Bay, Cuba. Whatever dreams Private Sandburg and the other men had of battlefield heroism were dashed when they arrived. The orders from Washington were confused, and there were no battles to be fought. When finally the *Rita* put ashore in Cuba, their most formidable enemies were mosquitoes, dysentery, oppressive heat, spoiled rations, and boredom. Charlie fought the boredom by reading his copy of *The New Webster Dictionary and Complete Vest-Pocket Library* and by writing long letters about the war to the Galesburg *Daily Mail.* The truth was that he had very little to report about the Spanish-American War. Five months after enlisting, Sandburg was back home with $122 in discharge pay.

COLLEGE LIFE

During his teenage years in the house on Berrien Street, Cully Sandburg met a number of people whom he would remember for the rest of his life. The one person who would influence him more than any other, however, was a man he had seen every morning but never actually met. Just before eight o'clock, a thin, bearded man with glasses walked past the Sandburg home lost in thought. He was Professor Philip Green Wright, later to become "a fine and dear friend" of Charlie Sandburg, "a deeply beloved teacher."

Cully's service in the military entitled him to free tuition for one year at Lombard College, and it was an opportunity he could not pass up. Lombard was the "other" college in Galesburg, with only 17 instructors and 125 students, much smaller than Knox. Associated with the free-thinking Universalist Church, the school had been founded in 1851 as the Illinois Liberal Institute. As its original name implied, Lombard was a decidedly liberal and innovative educational institution. It would be perfect for Cully Sandburg. The young veteran was accepted on only a provisional basis because he did not have a high school diploma. In the first year he enrolled for classes in English, Latin, inorganic chemistry, speech, and drama.

To pay for his food, clothes, and books, Sandburg took whatever odd jobs he could find. On campus he rang the bell to signal the beginning and end of each class period. The carillon tower was filled with dusty old theological tomes, and Charlie spent hundreds of hours reading about God, hell, and universal salvation. Never after his confirmation as a Lutheran did Sandburg belong to any established church, but his knowledge of formalized religions and his own personal faith stemmed in good part from his readings in the Lombard bell tower. Of greater importance to his immediate livelihood,

however, was his appointment by the mayor of Galesburg as a "call man" for the fire department. For ten dollars a month he slept in the firehouse at night, telephoned when the siren went off in the daytime, and hopped on his bicycle to help out if the fire was a big one. Later in his college career, Sandburg worked as a janitor in the Lombard gymnasium and as a door-to-door salesman of stereoscopic photographs (two-dimensional views which could be seen in three-D with a special viewer).

As hard as he worked and as much as he enjoyed his freshman year, Charlie was pleasantly surprised in May 1899 when he was offered an opportunity to attend the U.S. Military Academy at West Point. The U.S. congressman for Knox County, George W. Prince, had determined that one member of Company C would be allowed to take the entrance exam, and the two commanding officers both chose Sandburg. If he passed the test, he would become a classmate of Douglas MacArthur and Ulysses S. Grant III. Cully passed the physical with ease but, as fate would have it, failed mathematics and grammar. He returned to Lombard for the fall semester.

Not until several years later did Sandburg realize how fortunate he had been in being turned down for West Point. He probably would not have been happy as a cadet, and he certainly would not have had time for all the extracurricular activities he enjoyed at Lombard. He was the business manager and then editor-in-chief of the school newspaper; sang in the glee club; acted in a musical comedy; captained the basketball team for four years; debated for the Erosophian Society, once winning fifteen dollars in gold coins; founded a dance club; and even won the school checkers championship.

More importantly, had Sandburg gone to West Point he would never have come under the wing of Professor Philip

To help pay for his education at
Lombard College, Sandburg (right)
sold stereoscopic photographs.

Green Wright. And had he not worked closely under Professor Wright, he probably never would have become a writer. The admiration that Sandburg developed for his mentor was summed up in a eulogy he wrote in 1934:

> *Philip Green Wright will always be a momentous figure to me. . . . He was a man of great and versatile intellect, so versatile that he was indifferent to the species of greatness that requires acclaim. I had four years of almost daily contact with him at college, for many years visited him as often as possible, and there was never a time when he did not deepen whatever reverence I had for the human mind. . . . He was a great man and teacher in his profound influence on the potential young men with whom he came into contact.*

Later earning distinction as an economist in Washington, Professor Wright taught courses in English, mathematics, economics, and astronomy. Like his own mentor—the English poet, designer, and socialist William Morris—Wright was a man of many talents. He wrote poetry, essays, and even musical comedies. He loved art, classical music, and philosophy, and he had a degree in civil engineering. His hobby was designing books and printing them on a small handpress in his basement.

Professor Wright took a special interest in Charlie Sandburg because he recognized in the young Swede an intense social conscience and a potential literary talent. Wright himself was a member of the Socialist Party and strongly supported the efforts of farmers, factory workers, and railroadmen to organize into labor unions. His call for a new social order struck a chord with Sandburg, who had seen economic despair, social injustice, and oppression of the working class from Galesburg to Chicago to railroad camps all across the Midwest. As a laborer, hobo, and soldier, Charlie had developed his own strong convictions about capitalism, industrialism, the labor movement, war, and the need for a new

*Charlie Sandburg during his
student days at Lombard College*

democracy. Together, Wright and Sandburg studied the important political philosophies of the day—communism, capitalism, socialism, anarchism, and Populism. They read all the important books and treatises, and discussed each one at length. Sandburg maintained his belief that radical changes were needed in American society, but he also began to realize that the democratic system—based on the will of the people—was fundamentally just and worth defending.

Professor Wright also gave Charlie his first competent instruction in writing. Two other students joined with Sandburg in the "Poor Writers' Club," an informal study group that met Sunday afternoons in Wright's office to read from Twain, Emerson, Kipling, and Shakespeare, and to criticize each other's own efforts. Carl would also visit the professor at home to talk about Walt Whitman and other subjects in literature, politics, and economics. About his favorite student Professor Wright later wrote, "I do not remember that there was anything particularly distinguished in his appearance, anything that is to suggest incipient genius. He looked like one of the proletariat rather than one of the intellectuals. . . . He had seen a great deal of the world, some of it, I believe, from the underside of boxcars." The discerning professor also saw in Charlie a free-spirited restlessness, a yearning to wander and an unwillingness to be tied down. "Sandburg," he observed, "true to his Norse instincts, disdains harness."

It was perhaps that same roaming instinct that led Sandburg to leave Lombard in 1902, only a few months before graduation. His autobiography ends with the Spanish-American War and provides no explanation for his quitting college. It has been suggested that he lacked the required math credits to graduate anyway, that he tired of the college routine, and that he thought of a diploma as a commitment to middle-class complacency. There may have been some truth in any or all of these explanations, but all Sandburg ever said about it was "I felt the call elsewhere."

ON THE ROAD AGAIN

In the summer of 1902, as he had five years before, Charlie Sandburg took to "wanderin'." Again he hopped a freight train, this time heading east. The first stop was New Jersey, where he stayed only a short time, selling stereoscopic photographs door-to-door. Then it was on to New York City where, on the strength of his college newspaper experience, he landed a job as a police reporter for the *Daily News*. Permanent, full-time work was not what Charlie was looking for, however, and six weeks later he was off again.

Sandburg was on the road more than two years this time, writing down everything he heard and saw. Still unsettled at the age of twenty-four, he did know for certain that he wanted to be a writer. Wherever his wanderings led him and whatever work he took on, he always found time to read books of current interest and to write his own poetry and prose. Professor Wright received long letters filled with poems and compositions by his wayward friend. Charlie was back and forth between the east coast and Chicago, where he wrote for a Unitarian journal called *Unity* and contributed poems to a small, soon-defunct magazine called *Tomorrow.*

The incident that Sandburg recalled most vividly from his wanderin' days—and which in fact brought them to an end—occurred in 1904 at McKee's Rock, Pennsylvania. On a moonlit night, Charlie hopped a train in Philadelphia and made his way toward Pittsburgh. In a suburb called Wilmerding, he got off the train, bought breakfast for fifteen cents, and set out on foot. By the middle of the afternoon, he had reached McKee's Rock and needed a rest. An open coal car lay idle in the railroad yard, and the weary traveler climbed in. Five other hoboes had found the accommodations to their liking, but Charlie did not mind sharing quarters and fell into a peaceful sleep.

Suddenly came the sound of police whistles. Before he even remembered where he was, Charlie was put in handcuffs and removed to the Allegheny County Court House.

The charge was riding a train without a ticket. Though the coal gondola was not part of any train and had not moved a foot while they were in it, the six hoboes were to get no reprieve. When Sandburg was called forward, he announced to the judge that he had served in Cuba with the Sixth Infantry Regiment of the Illinois Volunteers. The judge noted that many veterans had passed through his courtroom but that military service was no grounds for dismissing the charge. The penalty would be a ten-dollar fine or ten days in jail.

Even if he had the money, Charlie would not have paid any fine. For the next ten days, he shared a tiny cell in the courthouse jail with two other prisoners. Until the day he died, Sandburg entertained the idea of suing Allegheny County for false arrest. For now, all he did was hop another freight train and make his way back to Illinois. His hoboing days were over, but they had provided a unique insight into the underside of American life. Later he would evoke them in his poetry and prose, never forgetting the loneliness and humility that had been a very real part of them. The poem "'Boes," for example, describes one stark moment in Sandburg's life on the road:

> I waited today for a freight train to pass.
> Cattle cars with steers butting their horns
>   against the bars, went by.
> And half a dozen hoboes stood on bumpers
>   between cars.
> Well, the cattle are respectable, I thought.

WORDS IN PRINT

In the fall of 1904 Charlie Sandburg returned to his job at the Galesburg firehouse. Clara and August little understood his comings and goings, but Professor Wright was enthusiastic about his future. Charlie had brought back a sheaf of new poems and compositions, and the professor thought they were good enough to be published. Under the stamp of his own Asgard Press, Wright printed fifty copies of a thirty-nine-page pamphlet called *In Reckless Ecstasy,* by Charles A. Sandburg. Each copy was hand-printed, bound in a cardboard cover, and tied with a red ribbon. The title was derived from a quote by the English novelist Marie Corelli: "Ideas which cannot be stated in direct words may be brought home in reckless ecstasies of thought."

Though a more mature Sandburg would be glad to forget his rough-edged first publication, *In Reckless Ecstasy* did evidence two of the chief interests of his entire life's work: the dignity of ordinary men and women, and the beauty of nature. "I glory in this world of men and women," he wrote, "torn with troubles and lost in sorrow, yet living on to love and laugh and play through it all. My eyes range with pleasure over flowers, prairies, woods, grass, and running water, and the sea, and the sky and the clouds." Also included in the pamphlet was a short essay called "Good Fooling," an appreciation of Abraham Lincoln. "Jollying is a fine art," it read. "The capacity for good fooling is an attribute of every beloved Master among men, and in proof history presents no more sublime and touching instance than Abraham Lincoln. My prayer is that I may be a good fool."

Wright printed two more works by the aspiring young writer: a thirty-two-page collection of short prose called *Incidentals,* and a sentimental ten-page poem, *The Plaint of a Rose,* with hand-painted flowers on the cover. Several of the essays in *Incidentals* demonstrated Sandburg's keen poetic sensibility and social conscience. He abhorred the violence of "bombs and brick-bats and broken skulls"; he affirmed his belief that strong individuals and great leaders would arise from the masses; and he held up Abraham Lincoln as an example of the common man rising to immortality. As for himself, Sandburg proclaimed a determination to understand better the startling beauties and ordinary mysteries of life around him. "I may keep this boy heart of mine, with tears for the tragic, love for the beautiful, laughter at folly, and silent, reverent contemplation of the common and everyday mysteries."

Having seen the vastness of life outside his small hometown, and with an unbounding curiosity, Charlie once again began to feel bored in Galesburg. He had seen his own words in print, and he longed to get on with his career as a writer. For several months he passed the time singing and playing the songs he had learned on the road. He quit the banjo and took up the guitar, learning to strum a few simple chords. Practicing the guitar became a daily routine, but finally Charlie realized it was time to move on. With a suitcase in one hand and his guitar in the other, Sandburg left Galesburg in the spring of 1905, never again to call it home.

CHICAGO

5

America in the first years of the twentieth century was entering a period of great social upheaval. Authors and journalists known as "muckrakers" were revealing the sins of capitalism and opening the nation's eyes to the brutal conditions under which many people worked. Union organizers were conducting massive drives to sign new members. President Theodore Roosevelt was doing everything in his power to bust business monopolies and institute social reforms.

The Midwest—and Chicago in particular—was at the center of this swirling storm of change. Jane Addams was running her famous Hull House, a settlement house that started a nationwide movement. Upton Sinclair's shocking novel *The Jungle* (1906) exposed the unsanitary conditions and exploitation of workers in the city's stockyard district. Frank Norris's *The Pit* (1903) was a similarly grim look at the wheat market. Socialist leader Eugene V. Debs, who had been jailed for the Pullman strike of 1894, spearheaded the American Railway Union (ARU) and ran for president of the United States five times between 1900 and 1920. In June 1905 "Big Bill" Haywood presided over the Chicago convention that founded the extremist Industrial Workers of the World (IWW), or "Wobblies." Radical newspapers and tabloids were sprouting up all over.

When Charlie Sandburg drifted into the Windy City in 1905, he was fully conscious of the social revolution taking place. He was in fierce sympathy with those demanding change, and it was only a matter of time before he would take an active part in the movement.

INTO THE FRAY

Shortly after arriving in Chicago, Sandburg was hired as associate editor of *The Lyceumite,* a periodical for platform artists. His main assignment was to write thumbnail biographies of performers and lecturers currently appearing around the country; he called his articles "Unimportant Portraits of Important People." On the side, Charlie also began giving lectures of his own. He had been reading a great deal of Walt Whitman and was fascinated by the poet's free-verse style and uniquely American message. He prepared a speech called "Walt Whitman: The Poet of Democracy" and delivered it with some success in Indiana, Michigan, and Pennsylvania. Other Sandburg lectures were called "Civilization and the Mob" and "Bernard Shaw: Artist and Fool."

In Chicago during the winter of 1907, Sandburg was introduced to Winfield R. Gaylord, an organizer for the Social Democratic Party. The Social Democrats were forerunners of the Socialist Party in America, and their single purpose was to promote a better quality of life for the working man and woman. Charlie was immediately won over and accepted Gaylord's offer of a job. A week later he left *The Lyceumite* and moved to Milwaukee, another center of the reform movement, where he was trained in political organizing. He plunged into his work with the zeal of a missionary, planning meetings, delivering speeches, circulating literature, and going on organizing trips to sign up new members. His district was the lake region of northern Wisconsin, where he addressed workingmen in nearly every village and town. He ate and slept in the houses of local party leaders, and he received only about twenty-five dollars a month by passing a hat after his speeches. The only other money he earned was from writing an occasional party pamphlet or an article for *La Follette's Weekly,* the magazine founded by Wisconsin politician and reformer Robert M. La Follette.

"Labor is beginning to realize its power," Sandburg told his audiences in those days. "We can no longer beg, we demand old-age pensions; we demand a minimum wage; we

demand industrial accident insurance; we demand unem-
ployment insurance; and we demand the eight-hour workday,
which must become the basic law of the land.'' Although
Sandburg produced an unending flow of polemic and commentary, he was less concerned with ideology than with the
actual living conditions of the poor and working class. Like
Eugene Debs, he espoused a ''socialism of the heart'' rather
than Marxist revolution. As a local recruiter for the Social
Democrats and a supporter of political reformism in Milwaukee and Chicago, he helped pioneer a new social order in
America—one that provides more for the greatest number of
people. His ''demands'' as a labor organizer may have
seemed radical in 1907, but within three decades, under
President Franklin Roosevelt, they indeed became the ''basic
law of the land.''

''LOOSING THE BIRDS''

In late December 1907, at party headquarters in Milwaukee,
Charlie met a pretty, dark-haired schoolteacher from nearby
Menomonee Falls named Lilian Steichen. The young woman
was on Christmas vacation from Princeton (Illinois) Township
High School, where she taught English. Miss Steichen was
visiting Wisconsin's Social Democratic leader, Victor Berger,
to discuss the translation of several articles from a German
newspaper. As Charlie soon discovered, the twenty-five-
year-old teacher with dark blue eyes was a woman of great
intellect who shared his passion for both literature and the
socialist cause.

Lilian's parents, a shop clerk and milliner, were Roman
Catholic immigrants from Luxembourg. They had not been
enthusiastic about putting their daughter through school,
hoping instead that she would take over the family hat shop.
But Lilian dreamed of becoming a poet and begged them to
continue her education. They finally gave in and sent her to
Ursuline Academy in Chatham, Ontario. After high school she
attended the University of Illinois for one year, only to realize
that more important work was being done at the University of

Chicago. She had developed a keen interest in the social problems of the day, especially child labor, and the outspoken social economist Thorstein Veblen was teaching at the southside campus. While at the University of Chicago, Steichen became an ardent socialist and was graduated Phi Beta Kappa. Her fluency in foreign languages and commitment to the cause prompted Social-Democratic party leaders in Illinois and Wisconsin to use her as a translator.

The afternoon of her visit to Milwaukee party headquarters, Charlie made it a point to escort Miss Steichen to the streetcar. They felt an immediate attraction and took up a steady correspondence over the following weeks. Lilian planned to spend her spring holidays at home in Menomonee Falls, and Charlie wangled an invitation. Lilian's hard-working parents were disappointed in their daughter's suitor, who dressed carelessly, carried union pamphlets and poetry books in his suitcase, and appeared to have no respectable career plans. The one family member who did take a liking to Charlie was Lilian's older brother Edward, a talented artist then conducting experiments with cameras, film, and developing paper. Edward Steichen would later become one of the great photographers of his time, as well as a close and lifelong friend of the poet Sandburg.

Lilian's nickname at home was "Paus'l," the Luxembourg word for "pussycat." Her friends had trouble pronouncing that, however, and called her Paula. Charlie thought the name suited her so well that he, too, took to calling her Paula. For her part, Paula thought the name Carl much more masculine than Charlie or Charles, and so from then on he became Carl Sandburg.

"So Paula," Carl wrote to her that May, "you have letters and letters to come—and we will send birds, love-birds with love-songs flying out over the world. We cannot live the sheltered life, with any bars up. It is for us the open road—loosing the birds!—loosing the birds!"

On June 15, 1908, when the school year was over, Carl and Paula were married at the Milwaukee home of a Social Democratic officer named Carl Thompson. No ring was used in the ceremony, and the promise to "obey" was omitted from the vows. Bride and groom made a solemn agreement that the contract would simply dissolve if either party wanted to end the relationship. Years later, after a mild spat, Paula asked Carl if he might want to invoke the agreement. "I'll be damned if I'll go through all that courtin' again," he replied.

The Sandburg's marriage was a happy union that lasted fifty-nine years, until Carl's death. All family decisions were mutual, and Carl often turned to his wife for advice on literary matters. He said on many occasions that the three most important influences in his life were Philip Green Wright, Edward Steichen, and Paula—though not necessarily in that order.

NEWSPAPERMAN, FAMILY MAN

The newlyweds set up house in a three-room upstairs apartment in Appleton, Wisconsin. At first all they could afford was a bed and mattress; Paula made cheesecloth curtains, and Carl brought home store cartons to use as a dresser. Now thirty and with the responsibilities of a family man, Carl had to think about earning a better living. In early 1909 the couple moved to Milwaukee where Carl took a job as an advertising writer for Kroeger's Department Store. Hoping to find newspaper work, he submitted six sample articles to the *Milwaukee Journal* and was taken on as a reporter. A few weeks later, he was hired by the *Milwaukee Daily News* as a fill-in editorial writer. It was only a temporary position, but one of his articles proved to be a turning point in his career. The Lincoln penny was minted in 1909 to mark the centennial of Lincoln's birth, and Sandburg wrote an editorial that attracted considerable attention. It was also the earliest piece of writing of which he could later speak with any pride. He called it "Lincoln on Pennies":

> *The face of Abraham Lincoln on the copper cent seems well and proper. If it were possible to talk with that great,*

good man, he would probably say that he is perfectly will-
ing that his face is to be placed on the cheapest and most
common coin in the country.

The penny is strictly the coin of the common people. At
Palm Beach, Newport, and Saratoga you will find nothing
for sale at one cent. No ice cream cones at a penny
apiece there.

"Keep the change," says the rich man. "How many
pennies do I get back?" asks the poor man.

Only the children of the poor know the joy of getting a
penny for running around the corner to the grocery.

The penny is the bargain-counter coin. Only the com-
mon people walk out of their way to get something for 9
cents reduced from 10 cents. The penny is the coin used
by those who are not sure of tomorrow, those who know
that if they are going to have a dollar next week they must
watch the pennies this week.

Follow the travels of the penny and you find it stops at
many cottages and few mansions.

The common, homely face of "Honest Abe" will look
good on the penny, the coin of the common folk from
whom he came and to whom he belongs.

When his two-week stint at the *News* was over, Sandburg
was hired back by the *Journal* as city hall reporter. In 1910,
with local elections coming up, Carl happened to meet another Socialist Party leader, Emil Seidel, who shortly thereafter
announced his candidacy for mayor. Sandburg became an
avid campaigner on Seidel's behalf, preaching his gospel at
rallies and on street corners. Seidel was swept into office and
promptly named Sandburg his personal secretary. Over the
next two years, Carl got a whole new education in the political system—from the inside. His main functions were to
schedule the mayor's activities, field complaints, and handle
the delicate matter of patronage. He could not—and would
not—commit any wrongdoing, but it was a fact of political life
that small favors were given in exchange for support. It was a
balancing act that Carl could never get used to.

In June 1911 Paula gave birth to the first of the couple's three daughters, Margaret. The need for a larger income and the distasteful aspects of his work at city hall prompted Carl to leave Mayor Seidel's staff a few months later. He was signed on as labor reporter for the *Milwaukee Leader*, the largest socialist newspaper in the state. Sandburg had a totally free hand, being allowed to write whatever he wanted. It was an ideal job for a crusading journalist, but again he did not stay long. An opportunity arose to work in Chicago and, even though it was quite indefinite, he could not turn it down. Chicago was where he wanted to be.

"CITY OF THE BIG SHOULDERS"

In the summer of 1912 a strike by newspaper pressmen forced the major Chicago dailies to shut down indefinitely. The only paper to continue publishing was the *Daily Socialist*, which changed its name to the *World* to attract a wider audience. Circulation jumped to 600,000, and additional staff was needed; Sandburg was one of several men hired from the *Milwaukee Leader*. That September, Carl moved with Paula and Margaret to a second-floor apartment on Hermitage Street on Chicago's North Side. No sooner had they got settled, however, than the pressmen's strike was resolved, the *World* lost its massive circulation, and Sandburg was out of a job. "I'd been broke before," Carl later recalled, "but this was different. I now knew something of the terror of an unemployed man with a family."

Though he could hardly have realized it then, the chain of events that brought Sandburg back to Chicago in 1912 would prove to be one of the most fortunate developments in his life. For it was in the "City of the Big Shoulders," as he would call it, that Sandburg finally came into his own.

After pounding the pavement for several weeks, Carl finally landed a spot on a liberal tabloid called *The Day Book*, owned by newspaper tycoon E. W. Scripps. The pay was only twenty-five dollars a week, however, and Sandburg did not feel he could adequately support his family on so little.

Swallowing his pride—and compromising his principles—he went to work for a conservative business magazine called *The System.* Although his salary was ten dollars a week more than at *The Day Book,* Carl could not get his heart into his work. He was asked to leave for injecting prolabor viewpoints into his articles; he had been ready to quit anyway. After a short stay at the *American Artisan and Hardware Record,* Carl went back to *The Day Book* and lectured on the side for extra money. Through it all, he remained active in Chicago's still-growing social reform movement.

Despite all his commitments, Sandburg also managed to find time for poetry. Late at night in the little apartment on Hermitage Street, Carl was fashioning a unique style of un-rhymed verse. He was reading a great deal of Walt Whitman and Japanese haiku, and he was writing as much as an entire poem every day. Paula, whose critical judgment Carl respected, had deep faith in the poems and sent them to magazines all across the country. There was no response for months, but Paula did not give up.

In September 1912, the same month that the Sandburgs had moved to Chicago, a woman named Harriet Monroe began publishing a small monthly magazine called *Poetry.* The purpose of the magazine was to feature works by little-known poets; over the next few years it introduced such names as T. S. Eliot, Robert Frost, Vachel Lindsay, and Rupert Brooke. Although the magazine was being published only blocks from the Sandburg's apartment, Paula did not even hear of *Poetry* until early 1914. She quickly sent out nine of Carl's poems, which ended up in the hands of Alice Corbin, Miss Monroe's assistant. Corbin was impressed by their originality and turned them over to her boss. Harriet Monroe picked up a poem called "Chicago" and read the first lines. She was shocked.

Hog Butcher for the World
Tool Maker, Stacker of Wheat
Player with Railroads and the Nation's Freight Handler;
Stormy, husky, brawling
City of the Big Shoulders

The more she read, the more Monroe realized that Carl A. Sandburg would be an important new voice in American poetry—powerful, simple, and unencumbered by rhyme or meter. The magazine editor took a deep breath, swallowed hard, and decided to publish the poems as soon as possible. All nine, with "Chicago" as the lead, appeared in the March 1914 edition of *Poetry*. Sandburg received one hundred dollars, the most he had ever been paid for anything, and the magazine could boast a new discovery.

Not surprisingly, reaction to the poems was loud and stormy. Readers accustomed to the flowery elegance of traditional verse were outraged by the use of slang and the lack of formality. Hog butchers and freight handlers, they scoffed, had no place in poetry. One respected literary magazine called the poems "an impudent affront to the poetry-loving public." More open-minded readers, however, quickly recognized the strength and vitality of Sandburg's free verse. Itself "stormy, husky, brawling," the Sandburg style might help liberate poetry from the prettiness and stuffy gentility of the previous century. For all the readers who found it crude and offensive, there were just as many who found it honest and refreshing.

TWO SANDBURGS

For Carl personally, publication in a prestigious poetry journal brought recognition and new opportunity. Things happened fast. At the end of 1914 he was awarded the Helen Haire Levinson Prize of $200 for the best poems published that year. He won acceptance into Chicago's most elite literary circle, meeting such writers and poets as William Butler Yeats, Edgar Lee Masters, Theodore Dreiser, and Ben Hecht. Arrangements were being made for more of his work to be published in another magazine, *The Little Review*. And in the fall of 1915 Alice Corbin took a sheaf of his poems to New York City, where she found an interested book publisher.

Alfred Harcourt, a salesman for the firm of Henry Holt & Company, had read Sandburg's work in *Poetry* and found it "stirring." When Alice Corbin brought him a whole manuscript, Harcourt "saw at once that it was of first importance and quality." Holt was a somewhat conservative publishing house, and considerable effort was required on Harcourt's part to convince the editors that the material was worthy. He succeeded. The collection was published in the spring of 1916 under the title *Chicago Poems*. Sandburg traveled to New York and met Alfred Harcourt, the beginning of a long business association and personal friendship. Harcourt would later become a major publisher in his own right, and Sandburg's books appeared exclusively under his imprint.

Carl dedicated *Chicago Poems* "To my Wife and Pal, Lilian Steichen Sandburg." The cover was designed by his brother-in-law, Edward Steichen, and featured an appreciation by Edgar Lee Masters. The author, it read, "sees with his own eyes, touches with his own hands, is hearty, zestful, in love with life, full of wonder."

Few volumes of poetry have ever been greeted with the attention and respect that *Chicago Poems* was in 1916. The critic for *Poetry Review* saw great natural beauty amid the shocking imagery. "Carl Sandburg," he wrote, "has shaped poetry that is like a statue by Rodin." A review in *The New York Times* called the collection "one of the most original books this age has produced." The reaction, however, was not universally favorable. *The Dial,* the same magazine that had called his 1914 selection an "impudent affront," now called Sandburg "gross and simple-minded."

The 146 works included in *Chicago Poems* at least should have proven that Sandburg was capable of greater subtlety and broader diversity than the blunt style of "Chicago." In "Skyscraper," for example, he brings out the "soul" in an ordinary building. He evokes a lyrical beauty in "The Harbor." And he creates a delicate imagism in "Fog." Louis Untermeyer, a noted literary critic and poet, once observed that there were really "two Sandburgs"—"the muscular, heavy-fisted, hard-hitting son of the streets, and his almost unrecognizable twin, the shadow-painter, the haunter of mists, the lover of implications and overtones." Nowhere is this better demonstrated than in *Chicago Poems*. Throughout the collection, Sandburg uses both voices to dramatize

his most vital theme—the yearning of ordinary people for happiness and beauty. In "Masses," for example, he starkly contrasts the simplicity and freedom of nature with the grim desperation of tenement life. There are hazy mountains and run-down streets.

Among the mountains I wandered and saw blue haze and
    red crag and was amazed;
On the beach where the long push under the endless tide
    maneuvers, I stood silent;
Under the stars on the prairie watching the Dipper slant
    over the horizon's grass, I was full of thoughts.
Great men, pageants of war and labor, soldiers and workers,
    mothers lifting their children—these all I touched and
    felt the solemn thrill of them.
And then one day I got a true look at the Poor, millions
    of the Poor, patient and toiling; more patient than
    crags, tides, and stars; innumerable, patient as the dark-
    ness of night—and all broken, humble ruins of nations.

A similar theme is developed in "Fish Crier," one of several poems in which the workingman finds satisfaction and joy in his life of labor.

I know a Jew fish crier down on Maxwell Street with a voice
    like a north wind blowing over corn stubble in January.
He dangles herring before prospective customers evincing a
    joy identical with that of Pavlova dancing.
His face is that of a man terribly glad to be selling fish,
    terribly glad that God made fish, and customers to whom
    he may call his wares from a pushcart.

*Edward Steichen took this photograph
of his brother-in-law around the time
Sandburg's first volume of poetry,
Chicago Poems, was published.*

AT HOME AND GOING PLACES

At the age of thirty-eight, Carl Sandburg had arrived. The publication of *Chicago Poems* marked the end of a long journey that had begun with his first eye-opening visit to Chicago twenty years before. Whatever the criticisms of its style, *Chicago Poems* established him as an important new poet and set him on the brink of a long and richly creative career.

By 1917 Sandburg had also found his niche as a journalist. In July of that year, *The Day Book* closed down because of America's entry into World War I; Scripps feared that the paper's socialist viewpoint would lose its appeal and might interfere with the war effort. Carl went to work for the National Labor Defense League, traveling throughout the Midwest to speak on behalf of striking union members. Then he was hired for a hundred dollars a week by the *Chicago Evening American*, owned by William Randolph Hearst. Within three weeks, however, Carl realized that he did not fit the Hearst mold and moved on to the *Daily News* for half the salary. For a variety of reasons, Sandburg felt at home on the *News*. He deeply admired its editor, Henry Justin Smith, and the staff of writers was one of the most impressive ever assembled by a newspaper—Ben Hecht, Lloyd Lewis, Paul Leach, John Gunther, Meyer Levin, and others. It was also the paper Carl had delivered every morning in Galesburg.

Sandburg's articles for the *Daily News* dealt primarily with the subject he knew best—labor. With the United States involved in World War I, union activity was not the major news. As a committed socialist, however, Sandburg did not think the two were entirely unrelated. In 1914, shortly after the outbreak of war in Europe, Carl had written an article for the *International Socialist Review* in which he maintained that soldiers were but exploited laborers: "It's a workingman's world," he wrote. "Shovels and shovelling take more time of soldiers than guns and shooting. Twenty-one million men on the battlefields of Europe are shovelling more than shooting. . . . The soldier is a worker, a toiler on and under the land." Now in 1917, with American soldiers being shipped off to battle, Sandburg broke with the Socialist Party line and supported President Wilson. On October 11 he wrote an item for the *Daily News* in which he criticized efforts by socialists to sabotage the war effort. The following week, Carl and Paula Sandburg both resigned from the party. Said Carl, "I fight against wars between wars, but once we're in it, I give it everything I have." He remained politically independent for the rest of his life, refusing to join any party.

The occasional opportunity to express personal opinions or promote social causes was only one of the reasons Sandburg loved being a journalist. More importantly, newspaper work immersed him in the day-to-day events that affected ordinary people in the city he loved. Some poets and critics suggested that being a news writer would tend to dull his poetic sensibilities. Carl felt quite the contrary. In verse as in prose, he was always concerned with real people, specific places, and true-to-life events. Working for the biggest and best newspaper in Chicago, he felt, gave him a special vantage point. It allowed him to experience the life and blood of the big-shouldered city—the fish criers, the skyscrapers, the toiling poor, and the blue burst of lake.

IN THE AMERICAN LINGO

6

The royalties and prize money from *Chicago Poems* helped pay the hospital bills for the arrival of the Sandburgs' second daughter, Janet, in 1916. The previous fall the family had moved from their second-floor apartment on Hermitage Street to a modest house in the Chicago suburb of Maywood. Although the extra income from his poetry and lecturing was a financial boost, the Sandburgs were by no means wealthy. Like his own parents, Carl and Paula ran a thrifty household. Carl preferred walking to taking a taxi, and he wore his suits unpressed; Paula dressed simply, though perhaps more neatly than her husband, and made every family purchase with great care. They referred to the first years of their marriage as "The Dark Period" (speaking only of finances), but even then they got in the habit of saving. Their goal was to make a secure future for their children.

A third daughter, Helga, was born in November 1918, and that winter the Sandburgs bought a large house in the western suburb of Elmhurst. The old frame structure was hidden by trees in the front, and a flat, open pasture stretched out behind. Carl and his family enjoyed the isolated rustic setting and called their new home "Happiness House." They led a quiet, serene life, the children frolicking on the living-room floor or the backyard lawn. Carl still worked late many evenings, but Paula would let the girls stay up to spend a few minutes with their father. After they had gone to bed, Carl had dinner with Paula and then went to his workroom to write. During the twelve years they lived in Happiness House, Sandburg produced eleven books of poetry and prose, and achieved the financial security to become a full-time writer.

CORNHUSKERS (1918) AND
THE CHICAGO RACE RIOTS (1919)

World War I was in its final months when Carl was sent to New York City to cover a labor convention for the *Daily News.* With his one free afternoon, he walked to the Hudson River piers where a troopship was just setting sail for Europe. Caught up in the patriotic fervor, Carl felt an urge to go with them. At the age of forty, he was too old to enlist, and the only way to get there was as a correspondent. As it happened, the Newspaper Enterprise Association, which provided feature articles for 390 papers around the country, had already thought of Sandburg as the ideal person to report from Sweden. Carl accepted the invitation and took a five-month leave from the *News.* In Stockholm, between October 1918 and March 1919, Sandburg sent long dispatches on the human side of the conflict and on the revolutionary turmoil then taking place in Russia.

While he was away, Henry Holt published his second book of poems, *Cornhuskers.* The contrasts between this collection and *Chicago Poems* came as a surprise to many readers. In subject matter, Sandburg had shifted his attention from the rough-and-tumble city to the windswept prairie. There was a smattering of poems about life in Chicago, but the majority of titles characterized the volume as a celebration of land, sky, water, and wildlife. Among them were "Prairie," "River Roads," "Laughing Corn," "Loam," "In Tall Grass," "Prairie Waters by Night," "Moonset," and "Goldwing Moths." In mood also, *Cornhuskers* was different from *Chicago Poems,* more sober and subdued, more meditative and perhaps more mature. Time passes, beauty dies and is reborn, seasons come and go; the only thing permanent is change itself. Sorrow and hope, regret and affirmation are stitched together to form the fabric of *Cornhuskers.* "Autumn Movement" captures the sadness of a passing season:

I cried over beautiful things knowing no beautiful thing lasts.

The field of cornflower yellow is a scarf at the neck of the copper sunburned woman, the mother of the year, the taker of seeds.

*The northwest wind comes and the yellow is torn full of holes,
new beautiful things come in the first spit of snow on the northwest wind, and the old things go, not one lasts.*

But the last stanza of "Prairie" is an expression of hope in the future:

> *I speak of new cities and new people.
> I tell you the past is a bucket of ashes.
> I tell you yesterday is a wind gone down,
>   a sun dropped in the west.
> I tell you there is nothing in the world
>   only an ocean of tomorrows,
>   a sky of tomorrows.*
>
> *I am a brother of the cornhuskers who say
>   at sundown:*
> *   Tomorrow is a day.*

The collection ends with a series of poems about an entirely different subject—war. Though they are among the grimmest and most powerful poems Sandburg ever wrote, the message is not unlike that of "Autumn Movement" or "Prairie": time and nature give perspective on the human condition. In "Grass," for example, they heal the wounds and cover the scars of senseless killing:

> *Pile the bodies high at Austerlitz and Waterloo.
> Shovel them under and let me work—*
> *   I am the grass; I cover all.*
>
> *And pile them high at Gettysburg
> And pile them high at Ypres and Verdun.
> Shovel them under and let me work.
> Two years, ten years, and passengers ask the conductor:*
> *   What place is this?
> *   Where are we now?*
>
> *   I am the grass.
> *   Let me work.*

As Sandburg knew full well, violence was not confined to the battlefield. Less than four months after his return from Sweden, bloody rioting swept the downtown area of Chicago. The problem had been brewing for years. Blacks living in overcrowded ghettoes and others migrating from the South in search of jobs had begun to settle in old, traditionally white residential neighborhoods. The city's expanding "Black Belt" created hostility and fear in the white community. The pressure intensified when white soldiers returning from the war complained that their jobs had been taken by migrant Negro workers. The time bomb exploded in late July 1919, when a black boy swam into the "whites only" section of a beach and was stoned to death by white children. Fighting broke out on the beach and spread to the streets. The rioting went on for three days, during which twenty blacks and fourteen whites were killed. In the Black Belt, homes lay smoldering.

Three weeks before the beach incident, Sandburg's editor at the *Daily News* had asked him to visit the Black Belt and report on the city's racial problems. It was Sandburg's last important work as a journalist, and probably his finest. His series of sixteen articles provided valuable insights into the plight of the black community and the causes of racial disharmony. "In any American city where the racial situation is critical at this moment," he wrote, "the radical and active forces probably are (1) housing, (2) politics and war psychology, and (3) organization of labor." Nearly half a century before the Civil Rights movement, itself attended by rioting, Carl Sandburg recognized the depth of America's racial problems and made a plea for government action: "The race question is national and federal," he maintained. "No city or state can solve it alone. There must be cooperation between states. And there must be federal handling of it."

In the winter of 1919, Sandburg's articles were collected into a book, *The Chicago Race Riots,* with an introduction by another liberal journalist, Walter Lippmann. It appeared under the imprint of Harcourt, Brace and Howe, the new publishing house established by Sandburg's friend from Holt, Alfred Harcourt.

*This Steichen portrait in 1919 captures
the strength and sensitivity of
Sandburg, the journalist, who at that time
was reporting on the Chicago race riots.*

SMOKE AND STEEL (1920) AND
SLABS OF THE SUNBURNT WEST (1922)

Shortly after his series on the race riots, Sandburg was asked to fill in for the *News*'s motion-picture editor, William K. Hollander, who was going on vacation. Two weeks later, Hollander announced he was quitting, and Sandburg was named as his replacement. Carl was no great movie lover, but he was pleased with the assignment because it would leave him more time for poetry. His schedule was arranged so that he could see five or six films on the weekend and finish his reviews by Monday night. That left Tuesday through Friday for his own work.

In October 1920 his third book of poems, *Smoke and Steel,* was published by Harcourt, Brace and Howe. The volume was dedicated to Sandburg's brother-in-law, with whom he felt a close artistic kinship. "To Col. Edward J. Steichen," it read, "painter of nocturnes and faces, camera engraver of glints and moments, listener to blue evening winds and new yellow roses, dreamer and finder, rider of great mornings in gardens, valleys, battles."

With only a few dissenting voices, the collection was well received. As the title itself suggested, the two Sandburgs—"muscular, hard-hitting son of the streets" and "shadow-painter, haunter of mists"—are very much in evidence throughout *Smoke and Steel.* The volume contains vividly real poems about workers in factories and fields, as well as more subtle works with vague implications and hazy, mystical overtones. The title poem, the first and longest piece in the book, combines both voices. It reads, in part:

Smoke of the fields in spring is one,
Smoke of the leaves in autumn another.
Smoke of a steel-mill roof or a battleship funnel,
They all go up in a line with a smokestack,
Or they twist . . . in the slow twist . . . of the wind.

•　　•　　•　　•　　•　　•

A bar of steel—it is only
Smoke at the heart of it, smoke and the blood of a man.
A runner of fire ran in it, ran out, ran somewhere else,
And left—smoke and the blood of a man
And the finished steel, chilled and blue.
So fire runs in, runs out, runs somewhere else again,
And the bar of steel is a gun, a wheel, a nail, a shovel,
A rudder under the sea, a steering-gear in the sky;
And always in the heart and through it
  Smoke and the blood of a man.
Pittsburgh, Youngstown, Gary—they make their steel with men.

In several shorter poems in the collection, Sandburg brings new insights to the themes introduced in *Chicago Poems* and *Cornhuskers*. In the search for happiness and meaning, he says, time passes silently and nature remains a mystery. The only answers come from within; the only recourse is to know oneself and be oneself. This was the harmony of Sandburg's own life and the message of many of his poems. "Purple Martins" is one example:

If we were such and so, the same as these,
maybe we too would be slingers and sliders,
tumbling over in the water mirrors
tumbling half over at the horse heads of the sun,
tumbling our purple numbers.

Twirl on, you and your satin blue.
Be water birds, be air birds.
Be these purple tumblers you are.

  Dip and get away
From loops into slip-knots,
Write your own ciphers and figure eights:
It is your wooded island here in Lincoln park.
Everybody knows this belongs to you.

For *Smoke and Steel*, Sandburg was named co-winner of the 1921 Poetry Society of America Annual Book Award, with Stephen Vincent Benét.

Slabs of the Sunburnt West, published in 1922, was among the most sympathetically reviewed—and quickly forgotten—collections of Sandburg verse. It was the smallest volume he ever published and probably the least inspired. In subject matter and style there was little that his readers had not seen before. The title poem is about the Grand Canyon, but many of the others cover old territory—Chicago and city life, the prairie and country folk, the moon, the sea, and "mist horizons." The style is predictably rough-edged, though perhaps quieter and less energetic than his earlier works. The book does include several poems of note ("Windy City," for example), but overall it had little that was new and exciting. The critics, at least, had finally gotten used to him.

ROOTABAGAS

Writing in 1920, Paul R. Benjamin in *Survey* magazine described Sandburg as having "a face arresting as Lincoln's . . . gnarled and furrowed, with granite eyes and steel gray hair. There is something artless about him," the article continued. "He has the uncanny directness and simplicity children possess." The playful spirit that endeared Sandburg to friends and strangers alike was also a vital ingredient in his literary style. The "boy heart" he had invoked in *Incidentals* was still pumping strong.

Having children of his own was a creative inspiration as well as a deep personal joy. Margaret, Janet, and Helga were at the age now that they begged to hear stories before going to bed. Carl read them fairy tales by Hans Christian Andersen, but he found little else that was suitable. So he made up stories of his own. In November 1922, Harcourt published twenty-five of them in a book called *Rootabaga Stories,* dedicated to "Spink and Skabootch," Carl's nicknames for Margaret and Janet. (*Slabs of the Sunburnt West* had been for Helga, or "Swipes.")

"I wanted something more in the American lingo," explained Sandburg about his stories. "I was tired of princes and princesses, and I sought the American equivalent of elves and gnomes. I knew that American children would respond, so I wrote some nonsense tales with American fooling in them."

Carl got as much enjoyment spinning his fanciful yarns as the children did in hearing them. The book opens with "Three Stories About the Finding of the Zigzag Railroad, the Pigs with Bibs On, the Circus Clown Ovens, the Village of Liver-and-Onions, and the Village of Cream Puffs." Others are titled "The Wedding Procession of the Rag Doll and the Broom Handle and Who Was in It," "How Bimboo the Snip's Thumb Stuck to His Nose When the Wind Changed," "The Two Skyscrapers Who Decided to Have a Child," and "How to Tell Corn Fairies When You See 'Em." The characters have names like Poker Face the Baboon, Hot Dog the Tiger, Henry Hagglyhoagly, and Jason Squiff. They all live in Rootabaga Country, where the sky is filled with peach, watermelon, and potato balloons; where clowns are baked in ovens and pumped to life with red wind; and where a monkey directs traffic.

So successful were Sandburg's "nonsense tales" that Harcourt brought out another volume in 1923, *Rootabaga Pigeons.* Both books were critically acclaimed, but to Carl that was incidental. The stories were a joy to create, and adults seemed to like them as much or more than children. Among the most enchanted visitors to Rootabaga Country was the famous architect Frank Lloyd Wright. "I read your fairy tales nearly every night before I go to bed," he wrote to Sandburg.

ABRAHAM LINCOLN:
THE PRAIRIE YEARS (1926)

In the back of Sandburg's mind through all his endeavors as a journalist, poet, and children's writer loomed the imposing figure of Abraham Lincoln. Since his boyhood days in Galesburg, Carl had been collecting books, articles, and anecdotes with an eye toward some day writing a more objective, in-depth biography than had yet been produced. By 1921 he had accumulated a wealth of material and had begun to organize it in files.

When Alfred Harcourt invited Carl to New York in late 1923 to discuss Sandburg's next book, author and editor were already of the same mind. In the course of writing his Rootabaga stories, Carl had got to thinking about the many biographies he had read in grade school—books about Washington, Napoleon, Julius Caesar, and other great leaders. It occurred to him that there had never been a really good young people's biography of Lincoln, and he resolved to write one. Harcourt, meanwhile, had had the same idea. An agreement was quickly reached, and Sandburg began work on what was to be a 400-page book for teenage boys and girls.

Two years later, Sandburg returned to New York to deliver a 1,100-page manuscript. Sifting through all his material had been like "operating a California orange-sizer," he said. "Certain material dropped out, other facts that were humanly interesting remained to go into the book. I found myself not guiding, but being guided by, the material." The more material he sifted, the more information there was to dig up. It had quickly become apparent that the book would be too long and too complex for teenage readers.

Abraham Lincoln: The Prairie Years was published in two volumes on February 12, 1926, the 117th anniversary of Lincoln's birth. The 962-page narrative begins in 1776, tracing Lincoln's ancestors back to Virginia, and ends with his departure from Springfield to be sworn in as president in 1861. In rich detail, Sandburg portrays young Lincoln growing up in Kentucky, Indiana, and Illinois. In a colorful and precisely drawn tableau, he highlights the personal qualities—wit, strength, courage, and compassion—that made Lincoln great. But *The Prairie Years* does not resurrect its subject as a mythological hero. Unlike any other biographer before him, Sandburg also describes the human weaknesses—stubborness, anger, and cunning—that Lincoln brought to his highest pursuits. Finally, recalling his own youth on the Illinois prairie, Sandburg brings to life the land and the people that molded the character of the Great Emancipator. In doing so, Sandburg relies as much on his own imagination as on historical documentation. One often-cited passage describes the home in which Lincoln's parents lived and the strange premonitions that came to his mother one year before his birth:

> The Lincolns had a cabin of their own to live in. It stood among wild crab-apple trees.
> And the smell of wild crab-apple blossoms, and the loving cry of all wild things came keen that summer to the nostrils of Nancy Hanks.
> The summer stars that year shook out pain and warning, strange laughters, for Nancy Hanks.

Several historians and critics took exception to such flights of fancy. The respected Edmund Wilson, for example, called the biography "romantic and sentimental rubbish." Others found minor factual errors, which Sandburg corrected in later editions. All in all, however, *The Prairie Years* was a huge success both critically and financially. "If the word 'incomparable' be given its literal meaning," wrote one Lincoln scholar, "only this book among the thousands which deal with the life of Lincoln deserves it." The *New Statesman* considered the work "a masterpiece which suits its subject," and *The Bookman* described it as a "veritable mine of human treasure from which to read aloud or to pore over by oneself."

The first forty thousand sets of *The Prairie Years* sold out in less than a year, but financial success had actually come months before the books were printed. The previous summer, Alfred Harcourt had sold the serial rights to *The Pictorial Review* for thirty thousand dollars. Sandburg was lecturing in Texas when he got the news. "Dear Alfred," he wrote back, "Thank you for sending a telegram with news equivalent to falling heir to a farm." *The Prairie Years* had made Sandburg a national celebrity; more important to Paula and Carl, it brought the financial security that they had long wished for their daughters.

THE AMERICAN SONGBAG (1927),
GOOD MORNING, AMERICA (1928),
AND OTHER WORKS

In the winter of 1926–27, in Santa Fe, New Mexico, for another reading and folksinging engagement, Carl again received an important telegram. This time the news was bad. His brother Martin, still living in Galesburg, wired that their mother had died. She was seventy-seven. On his way to Illinois for the funeral, Carl reflected on Clara's travails as a young immigrant. He was grateful for the fact that she had lived to see her children find success in America. Mary had become a nurse and hospital superintendent; Martin was doing well in business; and Carl was a famous poet and historian. August Sandburg had died seventeen years before, still worrying about his wayward "Sharley." Clara alone had the joy of seeing Carl's dedication in *The Prairie Years*: to his parents, "Workers on the Illinois Prairie."

Having spent two years almost exclusively on Lincoln, Carl began devoting time to other pursuits. The complete biography was his life's ambition, and he kept a close eye on his Lincoln collection. Over the next four years, however, Sandburg produced five new books wholly unrelated to Lincoln, as well as a twice-weekly column for the *Daily News* called "The Notebook of Carl Sandburg."

The first project was probably the most enjoyable and relaxing he ever undertook—compiling a book of his favorite American folk songs. Working with singers, musicologists, and folklorists, he assembled the music and lyrics into a volume called *The American Songbag,* published by Harcourt, Brace and Company in 1927. The book contains 304 folk songs, ballads, and ditties from all regions of the country; more than a hundred of them had never been published before. Each song is introduced by an author's note indicating where he heard it, the historical background, and special points of interest.

"*The American Songbag,*" he wrote in the book's preface, "comes from the hearts and voices of thousands of men and women. They made new songs, they changed old songs, they carried songs from place to place, they resurrected and kept alive dying and forgotten songs." As far as keeping songs alive, Sandburg's collection was itself an important contribution to American culture. The inspiration, as in all of his work, was the strength and wisdom of the people. Like *Chicago Poems* and his other free-verse collections, like *The Prairie Years, The Chicago Race Riots,* and even the Rootabaga series, *Songbag* is uniquely American in voice and spirit. It was a notable achievement in Sandburg's mission to find that special voice and give it meaning.

With each new book, Carl Sandburg gained further recognition as the mouthpiece of America. His reputation abroad was enhanced by the publication in London of *Selected Poems* in 1926. At home, awards and citations streamed in. He received honorary doctorates in literature from Lombard College, Knox College, and Northwestern University. In June 1928 he was honored as the Phi Beta Kappa poet at Harvard. Having never graduated from college, Sandburg was somewhat amused by the prospect of receiving a Phi Beta Kappa key, especially from an institution so prestigious as Harvard. He was flattered by the invitation to give a reading there and accepted with humility: "Harvard has more of a reputation to lose than I have, so I'll go."

The long poem he wrote for the occasion, "Good Morning, America," was vintage Sandburg. It is a catalogue of slogans and proverbs, and an evocation of natural beauty; it is a celebration of life and a reminder of death; a review of history, a dismissal of the past; an expression of doubt, an affirmation of hope; a loud reprimand, a quiet meditation. Man is a "little two-legged joker," says Sandburg. Fliers and fighters, pioneers and profiteers all return to dust. Generations pass, and the heart remains full of riddles. Yet life does offer pleasures; work, play, and the beauty of nature. And America does offer a promise: the joy of renewal. In looking toward the future, Sandburg concludes with the following prayer:

Sea sunsets, give us keepsakes.
Prairie gloamings, pay us for prayers.
Mountain clouds on bronze skies—
  Give us great memories.
Let us have summer roses.
Let us have tawny harvest haze in pumpkin time.
Let us have springtime faces to toil for and play for.
Let us have the fun of booming winds and long waters.
Give us dreamy blue twilights—of winter evenings—to wrap us
  in a coat of dreaminess.
Moonlight, come down—shine down, moonlight—meet every bird
  cry and every song calling to a hard old earth, a sweet
  young earth.

With "Good Morning, America" as the title poem, Harcourt published Sandburg's fifth volume of verse in the summer of 1928. Mark Van Doren, a prominent literary critic, wrote that Sandburg "knows better than any of his contemporaries how to put a flowing world on paper."

Good Morning, America was succeeded in January 1929 by *Steichen the Photographer,* a biography and appreciation of Carl's brother-in-law; in the spring of 1930 by *Potato Face,* another book of Rootabaga stories; and later in 1930 by *Early Moon,* a collection of poems for children. Now fifty-two, Sandburg had proven his skills in nearly all fields of literary endeavor—poetry, journalism, biography, children's writing, and folklore. He knew he had reached a crossroads, however, for his major work was yet unwritten.

Lincoln still loomed.

LINCOLN'S SHADOW

7

With the first royalties from *The Prairie Years,* the Sandburgs bought a summer cottage in the resort town of Harbert, Michigan, sixty miles east of Chicago across Lake Michigan. They spent their summers there beginning in 1926, reveling in the sun, the sea breeze, and the seclusion. For Carl, the peace and privacy made it an ideal place to work. His Lincoln collection was outgrowing the workroom in Elmhurst, and the house in Michigan had enough space to set up a library. In 1928 Carl asked Paula to choose between Michigan and Illinois as a permanent residence. She chose Michigan.

Under Paula's supervision, the Sandburg's built a new house suitable for year-round living. The three-story structure was in a row of houses spread across the sand dunes, overlooking the water. From the front porch, the family could see ten miles of beachfront through a cluster of pine and hardwood trees. Paula began raising dairy goats and built a special barn to accommodate them; over the years she became an expert breeder, selling her stock at state fairs and lecturing on animal husbandry at various universities. The Sandburgs dubbed their new home "Chikaming Goat Farm," after the Indians who had first settled the area. In May 1932 Carl left the *Chicago Daily News* and moved his family permanently to Chikaming.

"OH, LORD, IF THOU WILT PERMIT ME
TO FINISH THIS TASK . . . "

It was in 1928, at the age of fifty, that Sandburg resolved to complete his Lincoln study. Still somewhat fatigued from his work on *The Prairie Years,* he confined his research to spare hours between other, less demanding projects. He realized that it was a tremendous task and that he could not push himself as hard as in his younger days. Though it would take him nearly twelve years to complete, Carl did feel that the project had come at just the right time in his life. "Between forty and fifty I would have had more drive," he later admitted, "but less perspective, less understanding, and less experience. But had I waited until I was sixty, I would not have had the physical endurance to finish the job."

At the house in Michigan, Carl began more rigorous work. Before he could start the actual writing, however, it was necessary to do more research, organize all the material, and plan the book in minute detail. In the first year alone he pored through more than a thousand books on Lincoln, his contemporaries, and the Civil War. In addition, there was a mountain of journals, letters, newspaper clippings, documents, photos, and odd bits of paper. While researching *The Prairie Years*, Sandburg had perfected a rather unique but highly efficient system of filing. Separate envelopes were designated for the many facets of Lincoln and the Civil War that he intended to cover. Into each envelope went all the notes, clippings, and other material that pertained to the specific subject. There was one marked "Looks," containing descriptions of Lincoln's physical appearance; another was marked "Four score and seven years ago," for information about the Gettysburg Address; another was labeled "Religion." Carl made up hundreds of such envelopes, some overflowing with material and others with only a few scraps. Part-time secretaries were hired to type notes, and Paula and the girls did much of the filing. "Oh, Dad," he remembered them crying, "it's such a nice day out. Do we have to classify today?"

In his attic study, Sandburg routinely worked sixteen to eighteen hours a day. Finding that he was most efficient at night, he worked until the wee hours, slept late, and walked on the beach before returning to his labors. As he became more engrossed in the actual writing, it became increasingly difficult to tear himself away from the typewriter. His vision began to blur, and piercing headaches forced him to the old cot he kept in his study. "Oh, Lord," he prayed, "if Thou wilt permit me to finish this task, then Thou mayest have me."

No one could expect to endure so grueling a schedule for twelve months a year, and even Carl saw the wisdom of taking a few months off. From November to March he traveled around the country reading poetry, lecturing, and singing folk songs. At colleges and universities, concert halls and hootenannies, his native wit and easygoing manner created a close rapport with large audiences. He now owned six guitars, but he still concentrated on only two or three chords. He enjoyed singing for the public, but his voice was a hollow, haunting baritone. He wore rumpled shirts and never rehearsed, but his personal warmth and clever showmanship made him one of America's most popular entertainers. Above all, he projected his own love of music and song. "It seems like every day when I am at all in good health, I've got to sing," he would tell his audiences. "I've got to find the guitar and pluck a little at it, go over old songs and new songs, and as long as I live I am going to be learning songs."

In addition to a rest for his eyes and a break from his writing, the concert tours were an opportunity to collect new material on Lincoln. His engagements were scheduled for cities and towns in which a library, private collection, or other resource might provide information relevant to his project. Wherever he went, he sought out people whose parents, relatives, or family friends had known Lincoln or any of the people who surrounded him. His study would bring together all the information and insights he could gather from ordinary people in every part of the country. It was a research method uniquely suited to a biography of Lincoln and true to form for its author.

During the winter months, Sandburg also found time to write poetry. His style and subject matter during this period were deeply influenced by three factors: his work on Lincoln, his devotion to The People, and the ravages of the Great Depression. The year 1936 saw the publication of his book-length poem titled *The People, Yes*—a collection of folk wisdom, a proclamation of human fortitude, and an inspiration in desperate times. He described it as a "footnote to the last words of the Gettysburg Address." It was his favorite poem, and probably his greatest.

THE PEOPLE, YES (1936)

"Slang is a language that takes off its coat, spits on its hands, and goes to work," Sandburg once said. His fascination with the idioms, proverbs, and everyday expressions of ordinary people is nowhere more evident than in *The People, Yes*. The poem is divided into 107 sections full of folk sayings, slangy dialogue, anecdotes, tall tales, and character sketches, all tied together with a free-verse mixture of commentary, humor, and prophecy. There are quotes from a Mississippi River pilot and a farmer's wife in Minnesota. A girl in Cleveland asks "Papa, what is the moon supposed to advertise?" A boy in Winnetka, Illinois, wants to know "Is there a train so long you can't count the cars?" "What was good for our fathers is good enough for us," say Sandburg's people. "What you don't know won't hurt you." "Money is the root of evil." "Bring it home, boy. Bring home the bacon." "Where you from stranger?" And "Where do we go from here?"

The People, Yes is about Americans—how they talk, what they feel, and the spirit by which they will endure. It is Sandburg's testament of faith in democracy and his fellow citizens. Lincoln is an ever-present character, the will of the people a constant theme. With the democratic system suffering a deep economic and psychological depression, *The People, Yes* came as a timely expression of optimism. "The learning and blundering people," wrote Sandburg, "will live on." " 'The people,' " said the farmer's wife in Minnesota, " 'will stick around a long time.' "

Hope is a tattered flag and a dream out of time.
Hope is a heartspun word, the rainbow, the shadblow in white,
The evening star inviolable over the coal mines,
The shimmer of northern lights across a bitter winter night,

The blue hills beyond the smoke of the steel works,
The birds who go on singing to their mates in peace, war, peace,
The ten-cent crocus bulb blooming in a used-car salesroom,
The horseshoe over the door, the puckpiece in the pocket,
The kiss and the comforting laugh and resolve—
Hope is an echo, hope ties itself yonder, yonder.

   •   •   •   •   •   •   •

    The people know the salt of the sea
    and the strength of the winds
    lashing the corners of the earth.
    The people take the earth
    as a tomb of rest and a cradle of hope.
    Who else speaks for the Family of Man?
    They are in tune and step
    with constellations of universal law.

    The people is a polychrome,
    a spectrum and a prism
    held in a moving monolith,
    a console organ of changing themes,
    a clavilux of color poems
    wherein the sea offers fog
    and the fog moves off in rain
    and the labrador sunset shortens
    to a nocturne of clear stars
    serene over the shot spray
    of northern lights.

    The steel mill sky is alive.
    The fire breaks white and zigzag
    shot on a gun-metal gloaming.
    Man is a long time coming.
    Man will yet win.
    Brother may yet line up with brother:

This old anvil laughs at many broken hammers.
    There are men who can't be bought.
    The fireborn are at home in fire.
    The stars make no noise.
    You can't hinder the wind from blowing.
    Time is a great teacher.
    Who can live without hope?

In the darkness with a great bundle of grief
  the people march.
In the night, and overhead a shovel of stars for
  keeps, the people march:

                                    "Where to? What next?"

ABRAHAM LINCOLN:
THE WAR YEARS (1939)

Back at Harbert, Lincoln was coming to life. Except during the winter, Sandburg rarely left his study. His typewriter chattered day and night, and the manuscript pages piled into the thousands. By August 1938 he had completed the fourth and final volume, but ahead of him still lay more than a year of reorganizing, revising, and rewriting. Again he prayed for the strength to finish, but now also he began to worry. Perhaps the material had got out of hand. After all his painstaking effort, maybe the manuscript was too long, too complicated, too full of facts.

"Nobody will read it," he remembered thinking, "it's too heavy. And maybe I'll never finish it. My only satisfaction is that a great and lovable character has become a reality to me. My recompense is that I've been on a long journey with one of the greatest companions of men."

To put his mind at ease, Carl asked his old friend from the *Chicago Daily News,* Lloyd Lewis, to read the text and comment on it honestly. Lewis, himself an authority on the Civil War, had been in touch with Sandburg throughout the project and happily agreed to read the manuscript. He was awestruck. Never had he seen an historical biography so rich in detail, so sensitive to character, or so eloquently written. Lewis's only suggestion had to do with the ending. He felt it should be more like a symphony, the tragedy and grandeur rising to a climax. He urged Sandburg to rewrite the closing chapters and to take his time doing it.

Carl heeded the advice and spent that entire winter redoing his chapters on the assassination, the national mourning, and the burial. When he finished, he cried. "I was parting with him after all those years, like people who had

lived with him. When Lincoln died, for a time lights went out for me. The tears came. I do not know how a man could hold so many—and be unashamed as they ran down his cheeks an hour, two hours, more."

In the spring of 1939 Sandburg took his 3,400 pages of manuscript to the Brooklyn home of Isabel Ely Lord, a Harcourt editor. There Carl spent the next five months preparing the typescript for printing, reading proofs, captioning illustrations, and indexing. When the job was finished, Sandburg said to Alfred Harcourt, "This has grown into a scroll, a chronicle. There's one thing we can say for it: it is probably the only book ever written by a man whose father couldn't write his name, about a man whose mother couldn't write hers."

Abraham Lincoln: The War Years was published December 3, 1939—nearly twelve years after it was begun and more than fifteen years since Sandburg had started work on *The Prairie Years*. What was to have been a 400-page biography for young people ended up a six-volume, 3,500-page historical treasury. *The War Years* alone was more than 1,175,000 words, substantially longer than the Bible and all the writings of Shakespeare. "That son-of-a-gun Lincoln grows on you," said Carl to reporters.

The initial printing was 15,000 sets, but hefty advance sales prompted Harcourt to order another 14,000 for Christmas and Lincoln's Birthday. At twenty dollars apiece, the 29,000 sets sold out in a matter of months. *The War Years* was the crowning achievement of Harcourt's career as a publisher and Sandburg's career as a writer. Charles A. Beard called it "a noble monument of American literature."

In the attic study of his house in Harbert, Michigan, Carl Sandburg worked for twelve years on his prize-winning biography of Abraham Lincoln.

Henry Steele Commager called it "the greatest of all Lincoln biographies." H. L. Mencken called it simply "the best American biography."

Indeed *The War Years* is more than a biography of one man. It is an authoritative record of the most tumultuous period in American history. It weaves a detailed and colorful tapestry of events, personalities, landscapes, national moods, political maneuverings, war strategies, and historical meanings.

With Lincoln at the center, it recreates the struggle of a democratic people to preserve their freedom. With war as a backdrop, it erects Lincoln not as a martyr but as a symbol of democratic society—flawed but just, struggling against grave challenges but with the strength to endure.

At the same time, *The War Years* is a sensitive and thorough portrayal of Abraham Lincoln the man. During the first months of his administration, Lincoln is depicted as humble, uncertain, and even slightly confused by his power. He remains humble throughout, but as circumstances change he rises to almost dictatorial power through cunning and perseverence.

Political opposition, disloyalty within his cabinet, and the tragedy of war leave him tired and haggard by April 1865. His famous sense of humor is all but gone, yet he maintains his faith in the people and resolves to rebuild the nation. His assassination comes as a tragedy of epic proportion, a dramatic climax masterfully developed by a biographer who thought of him as both a friend and a paragon.

In writing *The War Years*, Sandburg drew on personal experiences uniquely suited to the task. The environment in which he was raised gave him special insights into the forces that prepared Lincoln for greatness. The stories of people who had known Lincoln personally were included throughout the book, and the prairie vernacular was authentically reproduced. Sandburg's descriptions of political infighting gained understanding from his first-hand experience in the administration of Milwaukee Mayor Emil Seidel. The accumulation and presentation of facts gave testimony to his skills as a journalist; the years he spent as a newspaperman were probably the best preparation he could have had for reporting the Civil War. Finally, his poet's ear brought to the work a beauty and lyricism rarely seen in historical biography. In many ways *Abraham Lincoln: The War Years* reveals as much about its author as it does about its subject. The final pages describe Lincoln's passing with a sadness that Sandburg felt as deeply as any person who lived through those times. His final appraisal of Father Abraham reflects the commitment to freedom and dedication to The People that both men shared. And his description of Lincoln's burial marks the end of a long personal ordeal. For Sandburg, as for Lincoln, there came a great quiet.

> To a deep river, to a far country, to a by-and-by whence no man returns, had gone the child of Nancy Hanks and Tom Lincoln, the wilderness boy who found far lights and tall rainbows to live by, whose name even before he died had become a legend inwoven with men's struggle for freedom the world over.

• • • • • • • • •

> Out of the smoke and stench, out of the music and violet dreams of the war, Lincoln stood perhaps taller than any other of the many great heroes. This was in the mind of many. None threw a longer shadow than he. And to him the great hero was The People. He could not say too often that he was merely their instrument.

• • • • • • • • •

> Evergreen carpeted the stone floor of the vault. On the coffin set in a receptacle of black walnut they arranged flowers carefully and precisely, they poured flowers as symbols, they lavished heaps of flowers as though there could never be enough to tell either their hearts or his.
> And the night came with great quiet.
> And there was rest.
> The prairie years, the war years, were over.

PATRIOT AND PROPAGANDIST

Carl had planned a well-deserved rest after publication of *The War Years*. He was sixty-one when the last words were written, and he had aged noticeably. The long years of exertion were etched in his brow, hung heavy under his eyes. With Lincoln gone there was a void in his life, and he looked forward to the simple joys of family, friends, and the windy beaches of Harbert. An interviewer asked what he planned to do next, and he replied: "I must first find out who this man Carl Sandburg is."

There was time for quiet relaxation with Paula and the girls, time for playing the guitar and helping raise goats, and time for reacquainting himself with Carl Sandburg. But one of the things he must have discovered about Carl Sandburg was that he could not rest very long. Too much was waiting to be written. Too much was happening.

In 1940, Sandburg was lavished with honors and awards as few writers in the history of American letters. He was awarded the Pulitzer Prize for history and elected to the American Academy of Arts and Letters. He received honorary degrees from Harvard, Yale, New York University, Wesleyan University, and Lafayette College, and he delivered the prestigious Walgreen lectures at the University of Chicago. He was featured in national magazines, and the Republican Party even tried to get him to run for president. In 1941 he received honorary degrees from Dartmouth, Syracuse, and Rollins College, and was invited to speak at meetings and conventions around the country. It was an embarrassment of recognition in which Carl would not have felt comfortable even in the most ordinary times. But now also he was preoccupied by far more serious matters—World War II and the debate over U.S. participation.

Since the outbreak of war in Europe, Sandburg had sided with the isolationists in opposing U.S. involvement. He prayed that Britain and France alone could defeat the Axis and that the lives of American boys could be spared. President Roosevelt, whom Sandburg deeply admired as the architect of the New Deal, had long favored U.S. participation in the war and had done everything in his power to help the Allies from a sideline position. Republican organizers who petitioned Sandburg to run against FDR badly misjudged his political convictions. Throughout the 1930s, Sandburg had been an enthusiastic supporter of the progressive measures instituted by Roosevelt to combat the depression. They were everything he had fought for in his own days as an organizer for the Social Democratic Party. In 1935, as he began the fourth volume of *The War Years,* Sandburg wrote a letter to his President: "You are the best light of democracy that has occupied the White House since Lincoln," it read. "You have set in motion trends that to many are banners of dawn." In 1940 the candidate of choice for certain Republican leaders was out on the campaign trail stumping for President Roosevelt. The title of his speech was "What Lincoln Would Have Done."

In June 1941 Sandburg had a change of heart regarding U.S. involvement in the war. France had fallen and Britain stood alone against the Nazi menace. The last hope for a free Europe was the United States, and Carl knew it. An isolationist between wars, Sandburg now realized that it was time to defend "our own way of life in line with the best traditions of Jefferson and Lincoln." FDR himself had already written to ask if he would run for Congress against the conservative Republican isolationist from southwestern Michigan, Clare Hoffman. "It would be grand to have your kind of Lincoln liberal on Capitol Hill," the president wrote. Sandburg, still not a member of any political party, declined gracefully.

From 1941 until the declaration of peace in 1945, Sandburg devoted his time and energy to promoting the U.S. war effort. He wrote and narrated radio scripts for the Office of War Information. He wrote an inspirational weekly column for the Chicago *Times* Syndicate. He wrote the commentary and captions for a photographic exhibit by Edward Steichen, "Road to Victory," shown at New York's Museum of Modern Art. And he produced an unending flow of pamphlets, speeches, poems, broadcasts, and other propaganda material. In 1943 a collection of them was published in book form, called *Home Front Memo.*

In his efforts to unite and inspire the American people, Sandburg called time and again on his old ally and friend, Abraham Lincoln. As in his radio broadcast of February 7, 1943, Sandburg invoked Lincoln as a symbol of faith, freedom, and strength of will:

The shadow of Abraham Lincoln spreads far—far enough to reach and touch in either sunshine or moonlight any place in his country kept sacred with meanings for the American people. His shadow lingers and the implications of his words haunt the national capital of Washington, D.C. and Pennsylvania Avenue and the clouds of misgiving and the rainbows of hope over the Potomac and the marble shrine at Arlington where in bright weather or blowing sheets of rain day and night the sentries keep watch as though over an altar of freedom where only the light-minded and those soft of faith have no hope for tomorrow.

REMEM-BRANCES

8

In the spring of 1945, as World War II was winding into its final weeks, a woman in Galesburg, Illinois, was undertaking a special project. Mrs. Adda Gentry George, the widow of a Northwestern University professor, had dedicated herself to memorializing the birthplace of the town's most famous son, Carl Sandburg. With the help of Carl's sister Mary, Mrs. George located the three-room shack on East Third Street in which Carl had been born sixty-seven years earlier. The dilapidated house near the railroad yards was now owned by a stubborn old woman who did not want it turned into a shrine. The woman died that fall, however, and her son offered a sixty-day option to buy. Mrs. George acted quickly. She launched an aggressive fund-raising drive and formed the Carl Sandburg Association to receive the donations. Before the two months were up, enough money was raised to buy the house, and renovations were begun the next spring.

On October 7, 1946—the eighty-eighth anniversary of the Lincoln-Douglas debate at Knox College—Carl Sandburg's birthplace was dedicated as a museum. Carl did not attend the ceremony, thinking it would be immodest to do so, but he did visit the site twelve years later for observances of the Lincoln-Douglas centennial. On that occasion he was asked if he had actually slept in the bed on display in the house. He promptly lay down on the mattress, closed his eyes, and announced, "Now you can say that I slept in it." More authentic memorabilia in the museum included the family Bible, the stereoscopic viewer that Carl used when he sold photographs door-to-door, and the Remington 15 typewriter on which he wrote part of *The Prairie Years* and some of the *Rootabaga Stories.* A special appropriation from the Illinois State Legislature paid for a separate Lincoln Room to house Carl's collection. Inside the front door of the cottage is a framed tribute from the poet Stephen Vincent Benét:

> *He came to us from the people whom Lincoln loved because there were so many of them, and through all of his life, in verse and prose, he has spoken of and for the people. A great American, we have just reason to be proud that he has lived and written in our time.*

REMEMBRANCE ROCK (1948) AND LIFE IN THE GREAT SMOKIES

Carl was far from done writing. In June 1944 he had signed a contract with Metro-Goldwyn-Mayer for "a biographical novel of American life, manners, and morals." Sandburg had for some time contemplated a "great American novel" that would span the nation's history from the coming of the pilgrims to World War II. Now with *Abraham Lincoln: The War Years* behind him, he was free to devote his time to such an undertaking. Always ready for a new challenge, he boldly went to work on the novel and published no other books during the more than four years he spent writing it. Though he followed his old routine, working late into the night and sleeping into the afternoon, his schedule was not nearly so arduous as on the Lincoln project. He worked only about eight hours a day now, compared with sixteen or eighteen during the writing of *The War Years.* Still, it was another ambitious literary endeavor that would require assiduousness and dedication. Nearing seventy, Carl had lost none of his drive, enthusiasm, or curiosity. "I never let a day go by without doing some writing," he said. "You know, you've got to let the hook down and float a sinker to see what's going on in the old bean."

Meanwhile, in 1945, Paula and Carl decided it was time to move from Harbert. They had endured thirteen harsh winters on the shores of Lake Michigan, and they craved a gentler climate. Paula also hoped to provide better grazing land for her goats. After a careful study of weather conditions and a trip to the Southeast that spring, they decided on the western part of North Carolina, at the edge of the Great Smoky Mountains. In a small town called Flat Rock, they found a large nineteenth-century, Southern-style house on 240 acres, called Connemara Farm. Though Carl would miss his walks on the beach, one look at Big Glassy, a 500-foot slope at the edge of the property, had him say to Paula, "This is the place." The irony of Connemara was that it had been built for Christopher G. Memminger, who became Secretary of the Treasury for the Confederacy under Jefferson Davis—Lincoln's counterpart and enemy. Noting another irony, Sandburg said, "Ain't it a hell of a baronial estate for a proletarian poet!"

That fall the Sandburgs moved into their new residence. Paula's prize-winning Nubbians and Toggenburgs were shipped express, as were Carl's books, papers, and other important belongings. Lumber was still in short supply because of the war, and all the bookshelves had to be brought from Michigan. At Connemara, every room on the main floor had fifteen-foot bookcases from floor to ceiling. Three items were never out of reach: a copy of Walt Whitman, a guitar, and a fire extinguisher. In the attic, of course, Carl set up a workroom. He indulged himself in a leather-and-chrome chair, but his typewriter still sat on a wooden crate. In this new study, Carl continued work on his novel, starting each day with a glass of goat's milk and a hike in the woods.

At Connemara, Sandburg
relaxes with his grandchildren
shortly before publication of
Remembrance Rock *in 1948.*

In 1948 Sandburg's fictional history was published under the title *Remembrance Rock*. It was more than a thousand pages, and Carl thought it could have run twice as long. The title refers to a large boulder in the garden of a former (fictional) Supreme Court Justice, Orville Brand Windom, who buries under it soil from Plymouth, Valley Forge, Gettysburg, and the Argonne Forest. Windom's narrative forms the book's prologue, and his own writings—discovered in a locked box after his death—provide the three parallel stories that make up Sandburg's novel. The first takes place in the early 1600s and recounts the ordeal of Pilgrim settlers; the second takes place during the Revolutionary War; and the third is set during the Civil War period. In the epilogue, Justice Windom's grandson has returned from World War II and buries beneath Remembrance Rock gravel from Anzio Beach, sand from Normandy, and volcanic ash from Okinawa—three of the war's major battle sites.

The three main stories are tied together by the reappearance of character types, physical traits, interpersonal relationships, and an engraved medallion passed from generation to generation. The recurrent theme is America's unyielding quest for greater freedom and fulfillment. Sandburg explained his work as follows: "The questions rise and weave and never end. How did this America we live in, the U.S.A., come to be what it is now? When and where did it begin and how go on? What is this elusive intangible, this mysterious variable that in moments seems to be a constant—what is this ever shifting and hazardous thing often called The American Dream?"

Remembrance Rock is, characteristically of its author, full of folk sayings and proverbs, finely tuned to the language of America. It is a sweeping panorama, often poetic, and with passages as moving as any found in the "great American novels." The critics, however, were disappointed overall— and perhaps justifiably. The less charitable dismissed it as "passing dull" and "not worth reviewing." The more insightful commented that "his portrayals . . . of American life are somehow static," that what each character "stands for" is too artificial and obvious, and that the book's artistic merits are drowned by its gushing patriotism. One reviewer suggested that it would make a better movie than it did a novel, but MGM never did attempt to put it on film.

THE NEW AMERICAN SONGBAG (1950) AND COMPLETE POEMS (1950)

Speaking to a friend once about critics, Sandburg drew the following analogy: "A man was building a house. A woodchuck came and sat down and watched the man building a house." More irritable on another occasion, he said, "It is a wonderful thing to be a poet and not a jackass."

Carl never paid much mind to critics, even the ones who thought highly of his work. By this stage in his career, his reputation could hardly be tarnished by woodchucks and jackasses. Having turned seventy in 1948, he could not be bothered by such matters. His experiment in fiction lay behind him, and there was still a great deal to accomplish.

In 1948 Sandburg accepted the honorary chairmanship of the Midwest "Freedom Train," an organization to collect food for war-torn Europe. He campaigned for Illinois gubernatorial candidate Adlai Stevenson, a longtime friend and mutual admirer, and made a fifteen-minute speech at Stevenson's inauguration. In 1949 Sandburg published a short book called *Lincoln Collector,* a commentary on the private Lincoln collection of another friend, lawyer Oliver R. Barrett. And in 1950 he produced *The New American Songbag,* containing forty songs from the original 1927 edition, dozens of others that had never before been published, and notes on the meanings and origins of each one. Carl had lost none of his passion for American folk music, still spending an hour or more every day singing and playing the guitar. It was about this time also that he began taking lessons from the famous Spanish guitarist Andres Segovia.

The most important event of 1950, however, was the publication of Sandburg's *Complete Poems.* The 676-page volume brought together his six published collections, in chronological order beginning with *Chicago Poems,* as well as a "New Section" containing seventy-two verses that were either new or had been excluded from earlier books. It was a compendium of all his work as a poet (so far), and it earned him another shower of honors and awards, including his second Pulitzer Prize.

ALWAYS THE YOUNG STRANGERS (1953)

If Sandburg had little patience for reviews and critiques, neither was he overawed by prizes, medals, or prestigious citations. He felt honored by the recognition, but he would dismiss them with good-humored flippancy. Preferring his quiet routine at Connemara, he graciously declined many a testimonial dinner. One award ceremony that he did attend was in April 1952, when he received the American Academy of Arts and Letters gold medal for history and biography. After the presentation, a newspaper reporter asked him what he was going to do with the medal. Remembering his life as a hobo fifty years before, Sandburg replied, "I'll wear it on the inside of my coat and when a railroad dick stops me and flashes his badge, I'll flash my gold badge right back at him." In fact, Carl had been spending a great deal of time recalling his experiences as a youth. For three years he had been writing a book about them.

On January 6, 1953, Harcourt, Brace and Company published Sandburg's autobiographical *Always the Young Strangers.* The book was conceived as only the first volume of Carl's autobiography, and it ends with his enrollment in Lombard College at the age of twenty. In uncanny detail, he describes his early life on the Illinois prairie—the visits to the Kranses, the suppers of boiled herring and potatoes, baseball and mumblety-peg on dusty streets, the county fair, the water pump and the ice harvest, Joe Elser's stories about the Civil War, the C.B.&Q. strike, the death of his brothers, George Burton's dairy barn and Humphrey's barber shop, the plaque on Old Main, John Sjodin, the Dirty Dozen, his first trip to Chicago, and the hobo jungles and boxcars.

But just as *The Prairie Years* and *The War Years* were more than a biography of Lincoln, so *Always the Young Strangers* is more than a nostalgic look back at Sandburg's own youth. He thought of it more as an account of "the life of a town and community, something of the life of the nation. If it should be called anything," he said, "it is the biography of a town filtered through the life of a boy." As much as a charming recreation of life in Galesburg it is a social history, a chronicle of the changes that came to small-town America as the nineteenth century was drawing to a close—immigration, industrialization, the labor movement. It is a book about the American experience, and the title itself is a statement of faith.

It is derived from a poem that Sandburg had written many years before, called "Broken-face Gargoyles." In that poem, he pins his hopes on "the young strangers, coming, coming, always coming." These are new generations strong enough and bright enough to overcome today's problems and forge tomorrow's progress. These young men and women, says Sandburg, seemed destined to be coming, always coming.

Always the Young Strangers was published on its author's seventy-fifth birthday, which was declared "Carl Sandburg Day" in Chicago. That evening a banquet was held at the Blackstone Hotel, and 550 of Sandburg's friends, relatives, and admirers showed up for the occasion. As the *New York Herald-Tribune* reported, it was really a nationwide celebration:

> *That Carl Sandburg's seventy-fifth birthday should have turned into a kind of informal tribute in a national celebration is altogether fitting to a literary man who, perhaps more than any living figure, is a voice of American democracy. . . . He is a kind of poet laureate of the people, collecting their ballads, commemorating their heroes, asserting their hopes, affirming their worth. Out in Chicago, they gave a big dinner for him, at which he jubilantly appeared with Lilian and his guitar.*

Governor Stevenson could not attend the affair, but he sent a recorded message in which he spoke reverently of his friend: "He is the earthiness of the prairies, the majesty of the mountains, the anger of deep inland seas. In him is the restlessness of the seeker, the questioner, the explorer of far horizons, the hunger that is never satisfied." Edward Steichen said of his brother-in-law: "On the day that God made Carl, He didn't do anything else that day but sit around and feel good."

Sandburg himself was the last to speak. "If I were sixty-five," he said, "such an evening would be difficult to take. If I were fifty-five it would be impossible, and if I were forty-five it would be unthinkable. But at seventy-five you become a trifle mellow and learn to go along with what true friends consider just homage."

HARD AS ROCK,
SOFT AS DRIFTING FOG

"Just homage" came abundantly in the last fifteen years of Sandburg's life. There was a gold medal from the Poetry Society of America, a scroll from the Civil War Round Table in New York, a $500 prize for poetry at the Boston Arts Festival, the Humanities Award from New York's Albert Einstein College of Medicine, the International United Poets Award as "Honorary Poet Laureate of the U.S.A.," designation as "Honorary Ambassador" of North Carolina, and honorary degrees from several colleges and universities. In November 1956, the first of sixteen public schools to be named after him was opened in Harvey, Illinois. In September 1964 he was awarded the Presidential Medal of Freedom by President Lyndon Johnson. And the following year, he became the first white person to receive the Medal of Honor of the National Association for the Advancement of Colored People (NAACP) as "a leading prophet for civil rights in our time." That award meant more to him than two Pulitzer Prizes.

The year 1959 was an especially eventful one for Carl. February 12 was the sesquicentennial (150th anniversary) of the birth of Abraham Lincoln, and Sandburg was invited to address a special joint session of Congress. Not since the historian George Bancroft had delivered a eulogy for President Lincoln in 1865 had any private citizen been so honored. His silver forelocks draped over one eyebrow, he stepped to the rostrum and scanned his solemn audience—senators and congressmen, Supreme Court justices, presidential cabinet members, and the Washington diplomatic corps. The Speaker of the House had introduced him as the person who knew more about Lincoln than any person alive, but as Sandburg spoke it became clear that he was more than that. Here was Lincoln's shadow, the personification of his character and the voice of his democratic ideals:

Not often in the story of mankind does a man arrive on earth who is both steel and velvet, who is hard as rock and soft as drifting fog, who holds in his heart and mind the paradox of terrible storm and peace unspeakable and perfect. Here and there across centuries come reports of men alleged to have these contrasts. And the incomparable Abraham Lincoln, born one hundred and fifty years ago this day, is an approach if not a perfect realization of this character.

•　　•　　•　　•　　•　　•　　•

Today we may say, perhaps, that the well-assured and most enduring memorial to Lincoln is invisibly there, today and tomorrow, and for a long time yet to come. It is there in the hearts of lovers of liberty, men and women— this country has always had them in crisis—men and women who understand that wherever there is freedom there have been those who fought, toiled, and sacrificed for it.

Several months later, the esteemed—but always fun-loving—historian and poet made a national television appearance on "The Ed Sullivan Show," reading some of his poems and strumming his guitar as Gene Kelly danced to the rhythm. At about this time also, stage director Norman Corwin was putting together a show based on Sandburg's poet-

ry and prose, *The World of Carl Sandburg,* starring Bette Davis and Gary Merrill. After a successful opening in Portland, Maine, the production toured seventy-seven cities and towns, including Los Angeles, New York, Chicago, and, finally, Flat Rock, North Carolina.

In the summer of the same year, Sandburg and Edward Steichen traveled to Moscow under the auspices of the U.S. State Department for the opening of the "Family of Man" photographic exhibition. Steichen had created the show in 1955 for the Museum of Modern Art in New York City, where he was Director of Photography. The exhibit consisted of 503 pictures from 68 countries taken by 273 amateur and professional photographers. The title, suggested by Sandburg, was a phrase Lincoln had used in several speeches and letters. The purpose of the collection was to depict the experiences, needs, and emotions shared by people all over the world. Sandburg wrote captions and a prologue for the exhibition, which had also been made into a book (1955).

On their way home from the Soviet Union, Sandburg and Steichen made a ten-day stop in Sweden. At Stockholm Airport, Carl greeted a crowd of well-wishers in the language of his parents. Swedish-American Day was celebrated on August 6, and thousands turned out to welcome the 81-year-old poet. That afternoon, and again in the evening on television, Sandburg read in Swedish the last letter his mother had ever written. A few days later he received the "Litteris et Artibus" gold medal from King Gustav VI for accomplishments in the fine arts, an award rarely bestowed on a foreigner. The real purpose of Carl's visit, however, was to see the villages in which his parents had been born. Making his way

Carl Sandburg spoke to a joint session of Congress and distinguished guests on the 150th anniversary of Lincoln's birth.

southwest from Stockholm, Sandburg (and a motorcade of reporters) came first to Asbo, the birthplace of August Danielsson. From there it was only a few miles to Appuna and the tiny farmhouse in which Clara Andersdotter had lived until the age of twenty-two. Before leaving the house, Carl stopped in front of a mirror in the hallway, looked himself straight in the eye, and whispered, "What on earth do you lack, boy?"

"WHERE I GO FROM HERE AND NOW"

Much as he hated to admit it, advancing years had finally forced Sandburg to slow his pace. In his seventies he gave up cigars and limited his whiskey to a small amount every few days. On his eightieth birthday he was asked what he missed most about being fifty. "Running up stairs," he answered. His "boy heart" was still intact, however, and Carl was happy for any new challenge. So in July 1960, at the age of eighty-two, he set out for Hollywood to be the dialogue adviser on Twentieth Century–Fox's film *The Greatest Story Ever Told.* "Why ain't I got a right to write for movies?" he demanded. "That's a high dive I haven't made yet. Why ain't I got a right to take a dive in the Twentieth Century lot?"

Back in Connemara, Carl was still working a few hours every day (still trying to "see what's going on in the old bean"), but for several years he had confined himself largely to introductions for other people's books and to new anthologies and condensed versions of his own earlier books. *Abraham Lincoln: The Prairie Years and The War Years* (1954) was a single-volume condensation of the monumental biography; *Prairie-Town Boy* (1955) was a children's version of *Always the Young Strangers; The Sandburg Range* (1957) was a general anthology; and *Harvest Poems 1910–1960* was a paper-bound volume for children. Among the many books for which he wrote a forword or introduction was *To Turn the Tide* (1962), a collection of speeches by John F. Kennedy.

When Paula didn't answer the door herself, visitors to Connemara were greeted by a slightly stooped, white-haired figure who answered the knock in huffy impatience. The sleeves were usually rolled up, and still-alert hazel eyes peered out from under a green visor. Few would have thought that he was working on anything important, but the fact was that Carl was writing one last collection of poems.

Honey and Salt was published on Sandburg's eighty-fifth birthday in January 1963. The book consisted of seventy-seven new poems celebrating love, life, and the land. It was in many ways the old Sandburg—blending rock-hard images and fog-soft lyricism, wry wit, and childlike wonderment—but it also showed just how much his vision and his sensibility had matured since he wrote about "hog butchers" and "freight handlers." The poems are more tender and reflective, delighting in simple sights, smells, and sounds from the perspective of old age. Finally, *Honey and Salt* is about birth, death, the "hush of time," and the natural harmony among all living things. In the last and longest poem, "Timesweep," Sandburg declares his kindred spirit and shared origin with the first splitting cells, the little fish, the big fish, earthworms, snails, pelicans and crows, crickets and grasshoppers, squirrels, goats, horses and bears, "blue-rumped baboons, chattering chimpanzees, and leering orangoutangs." He is all of these, he says, and they are all a part of him. They are his origin and his pedigree.

> *I am more than a traveler out of Nowhere.*
> *Sea and land, sky and air, begot me Somewhere.*
> *Where I go from here and now, or if I go at all*
> *again, the Maker of sea and land, of sky and*
> *air, can tell.*

> *There is only one horse on earth*
> *and his name is All Horses.*
> *There is only one bird in the air*
> *and his name is All Wings.*
> *There is only one fish in the sea*
> *and his name is All Fins.*
> *There is only one man in the world*
> *and his name is All Men.*

There is only one woman in the world
and her name is All Women.
There is only one child in the world
and the child's name is All Children.
   There is only one Maker in the world
   and His children cover the earth
   and they are named All God's Children.

Four and a half years later—quiet years with Paula at Connemara—on July 22, 1967, Sandburg died peacefully in his
sleep. The body was cremated, and the ashes were sprin-
kled under a granite boulder—"Remembrance Rock"—
behind the three-room cottage on East Third Street in Galesburg. "It was his idea," said Paula.

LITERARY
LIBERTY BELL

9

It was in 1896, after his first glimpse of life outside Galesburg, that Cully Sandburg decided what he wanted to do in life. "I'm going away," he told his older sister. "I'm going to be a writer."

In the "Notes for a Preface" to his *Complete Poems*, 72-year-old Carl Sandburg looked back on his career and reaffirmed his commitment:

> *I have written by different methods and in a wide miscellany of moods and have seldom been afraid to travel in lands and seas where I met fresh scenes and new songs. All my life I have been trying to learn and read, to see and hear, and to write. At sixty-five I began my first novel, and the five years lacking a month I took to finish it, I was still traveling, still a seeker. I should like to think that as I go on writing there will be sentences truly alive, with verbs quivering, with nouns giving color and echoes. It could be, in the grace of God, I shall live to be eighty-nine, as did Hokusai, and speaking my farewell to earthly scenes, I might paraphrase: "If God had let me live five years longer I should have been a writer."*

Sandburg lived to the age of eighty-nine, but he had been a writer—a versatile, prolific, and highly distinctive one—for more than half a century. There are successes and failures among his works, important books that are still of interest and insignificant ones that are ignored. Of his prose works, the Lincoln opus and *Always the Young Strangers* stand out as American classics. As for his poetry, future interest will depend largely on the tastes and preferences of individual readers. For Sandburg as for few other poets, critical judgment is taken out of the hands of "experts" and left to the reading public. Simple construction, straightforward language, and unobscure messages make his poems intelligible to a wide "nonliterary" audience. His achievement as a poet was to bring an increasingly elitist art form into the common realm, to reanimate it with a human touch. If any American poet has been read by more people than Carl Sandburg, certainly none has been read—and loved—by as many different *kinds* of people.

Sandburg injected humanity into his writing by injecting himself into it. More so than for most other writers, his own character and personal experiences are reflected in his style. He grew up among ordinary working people, and he wrote about them from their own point of view and in their own language. His poems are as free-spirited and unpolished as his own personality. They wander and ramble as once Sandburg rambled around the country; they make inventories of life rather than self-assured pronouncements. They ponder and pose questions, leaving fate for others to determine. His prose style is breezy and lyrical, but governing it are the eyes of a reporter, the mind of a socialist, and the heart of a staunch patriot. There is an authentic quality to everything he wrote, a natural wit and warmth, a thorough and abiding faith. Above all, there is a sense of shared human experience and shared hope. This is the spirit of *The Family of Man:*

> *People! flung wide and far, born into toil, struggle, blood and dreams, among lovers, eaters, drinkers, workers, loafers, fighters, players, gamblers. Here are ironworkers, bridgemen, musicians, sandhogs, miners, builders of huts and skyscrapers, jungle hunters, landlords and the landless, the loved and the unloved, the lonely and the abandoned, the brutal and the compassionate—one big family hugging close to the ball of Earth for its life and being.*

Sandburg's friend Harry Golden once asked him about his religious beliefs. The reply? "I am a Christian, a Quaker, a Moslem, a Buddhist, a Shintoist, a Confucian, and maybe a Catholic pantheist or a Joan of Arc who hears voices—I am all of these and more. Definitely I have more religions than I have time or zeal to practice in true faith." Fully a third of all the poems he ever wrote, it has been noted, make some allusion to God, religion, or the Bible. Others take the form of a solemn meditation or prayer. Formalized religion played no role in his personal life, and theological doctrine found no expression in his writings. At the center of both, however, lay the passion, wonder, ethical fervor, and faith in goodness and beauty basic to any religious orthodoxy. He wondered about the things that people everywhere wonder about—the sun, moon, and stars, the passing of time, and the meaning of life and death—and he prayed for the things that people everywhere pray for—sustenance, joy, harmony, and hope.

In his own life, Sandburg lived out the faith at the core of his writings—the equality of all and the beauty of the life of the common man and woman. He dressed like one and spoke like one, took joy in their music, and fought for their rights. Just as he belonged to no church, so he would join no political party. But just as he prayed for hope and harmony, so he battled for social justice. Possessed of a stubborn social conscience, he championed the causes of unionism, civil rights, and aid for the poor. His political views as a youth were considered radical, but they became the mainstream within a few short decades. Despite his sometimes fierce social criticisms, Sandburg was also a passionate and thoroughgoing patriot. When his country came up against the Nazi-Japanese threat in World War II, he was an enthusiastic and unabashed propagandist. There was no inconsistency or

Carl Sandburg's poetry reflected the warmth and humanity that shone through his own life.

—115—

contradiction between his social criticism and his patriotism, however, no reversal of thinking or shift in attitude. From his days as a socialist organizer to his work for the Office of War Information, he was advocating and defending a true democracy—of, by, and for the people.

No more than he had joined any church or political party, Sandburg subscribed to no formal school or style of writing. His purpose was to find a voice and style appropriate for America and Americans in the twentieth century. As social and economic changes were bringing greater freedom and equality for all classes, so literature had to be freed from old doctrines and outdated standards. "It is a time of confusions. Particularly in America is it a period of chaos," wrote Sandburg in 1922. "Art today, if it is to get results, must pierce exteriors and surfaces by ways different from artists or older times." Rejecting what he called "Arrow Collar" literature, Sandburg resorted to a free-verse style and the idioms of the provincial working class. Some said his slangy, rambling compositions weren't "poetry" at all, but he probably didn't care much what they called it. Accused of writing without form, he told an interviewer, "Well, I'm not some sort of *addict* for form. But if I lack form, all the proverbs of Solomon, all the psalms of David, the book of Ecclesiastes, and the Old Testament—they are all lacking form."

It is true that some of Sandburg's poems have lost their timeliness and impact. It is true that free verse has itself been replaced by new styles and techniques. And it is true that some of his prose works are of only historical interest. In the final analysis, however, it can only be concluded that Carl Sandburg made important and permanent contributions to American literature and life. His disregard for established verse forms, and the color and vitality of his own style, helped bring on a new era in poetry. His portraits of rural and urban life built a bridge between nineteenth-century frontierism and twentieth-century industrialism. He recorded the history and folklore of the nation, articulated its values and ideals. Above all, he gave an authentic human voice to its people—all of its people. His literature, like his politics, was in the spirit of a true democracy—of, by, and for the people.

If the purpose of a writer is to entertain and inspire with words, to bring new insights to life and the world around us, and to fashion the language of a people and a time, then Carl Sandburg fulfilled the dream he had spoken to his sister Mary that afternoon in 1896. His accomplishments as a writer and his impact on the American scene were summarized in a *New York Times* editorial on the occasion of his seventy-fifth birthday:

> *He is more than a poet, biographer, historian, more than a man of infinitely entertaining and moving words. Child of Swedish parents, son of the Middle West, epic interpreter of Abraham Lincoln, poet laureate of Chicago, he has been a kind of literary Liberty Bell ringing across the prairies and the decades. His poetry often breaks into prose, his prose often heightens into poetry, but the rich imagery, the sensitiveness, the pity, and the humor are never lacking. . . . He has never been a poseur, never self-conscious, never pretentious. He has been honestly a seeker, never sure what he sought he has found or will ever find.*

FOR FURTHER READING

For anyone interested in the life and craft of Carl Sandburg, there is no substitute for Sandburg's own writings. Recommended for almost any reader is *Always the Young Strangers,* a vivid and highly entertaining account of his first twenty years; *Prairie-Town Boy* is a condensed children's version. Unsurpassed for its insights into the man and his vision is, of course, *The Complete Poems of Carl Sandburg* (revised and expanded edition, 1970); this is a volume to which one can return for a lifetime and always find new pleasures. For those who have the time and ambition, *Abraham Lincoln: The Prairie Years* and *Abraham Lincoln: The War Years* will be richly rewarding; for those who do not, a condensed combined edition can be found in most libraries. In addition to the other titles mentioned in this book, *The Letters of Carl Sandburg,* edited by Herbert Mitgang, is readable and revealing.

Among the many biographies, appreciations, and commentaries written by others, Harry Golden's *Carl Sandburg* stands out for its colorful anecdotes and warm personal remembrances. *Carl Sandburg—A Pictorial Biography,* by Joseph Haas and Gene Lovitz, combines a lively text with 160 photographs of Sandburg, his family and friends, and the places he lived. *Carl Sandburg—Lincoln of Our Literature,* by North Callahan, is a good general biography. Richard Crowder's *Carl Sandburg* and Gay Wilson Allen's *Carl Sandburg* (University of Minnesota Pamphlets on American Writers) focus on the Sandburg poetry and give useful insights. Helga Sandburg recalls her parents in *A Great & Glorious Romance—The Story of Carl Sandburg and Lilian Steichen.*

INDEX